Ministry
in a
DISASTER ZONE

To Minister Salathiel McDonald,

Be Blessed!

Published by
ACB Ministry @ Mount Lebanon Baptist Church
Brooklyn, NY

Ministry in a DISASTER ZONE

The Seven Cross-Sayings of
Jesus as Preached at
An African American Urban Church
(The Saint Paul Community Baptist Church
Brooklyn, New York)

by ALVIN C. BERNSTINE

Foreword by
Rev. Dr. Johnny Ray Youngblood

Cover Photo Courtesy of New York Police Department

Published by ACB Ministry @ Mount Lebanon Baptist Church, 230 Decatur Street, Brooklyn, NY 11233

Distributed by Ingram Book Group of Ingram Publications (USA) and Amazon.com

Layout & Design by Written Expressions Enterprise, Inc., 2276 Griffin Way, Suite 105-161, Corona, CA 92879; (951) 371-0160; www.writtenexpressions.com

ISBN: 0-9767020-0-2

FIRST EDITION

Library of Congress: Pending

Printed in the United States of America by Lightning Source Incorporated, 1246 Heil Quaker Boulevard, La Vergue, TN 37086

Dedicated to the memory of
Dr. Samuel Dewitt Proctor –
A saint, a scholar, a wonderful gift
to the human race.

Thanks Doc for teaching
us all how to preach.

CONTENTS

FOREWORD

No brighter light shines in the American pulpit today, neither black nor white, than Alvin C. Bernstine. It has been the privilege of the pastor and people of the St. Paul Community Baptist Church of Brooklyn, New York to sit at the feet of this matchless sermonizer for the past eight years.

The Good Friday preaching series has been qualified and defined by the preaching of Alvin C. Bernstine. Bernstine's insight is unique, compelling and inarguable. He is a true exegete and his application is astounding. Bernstine argues like a lawyer. He logicizes with the profundity of a philosopher and convicts like a cutting edge sword.

The declaration of Calvary as a "disaster zone" and the recognition of the words and ways of Jesus on that cross as ministry is nothing short of "HOPEFUL". All seven of these words as addressed by and filtered through the mind of Alvin Bernstine are a must for repetition or pump priming. Particularly, provocative to me is the message of the Third Word: "Woman Behold Thy Son, Son Behold Thy Mother". Every warrior-preacher needs to have this collection of messages from this brother whose faithfulness and thoroughness

i

in text preparation for preaching is at points enviable.

I trust that this set of sermons is the first in a volume to one day be called "The Best of Bernstine". I thank God for this preacher.

Rev. Dr. Johnny Ray Youngblood, Senior Pastor
St. Paul Community Baptist Church
Brooklyn, NY

ACKNOWLEDGEMENTS

Special thanks to Cobertha Felix, who faithfully coordinates ACB Ministry, Monica Jackson of Written Expressions Enterprise, Inc., who provided invaluable professional assistance. A special thanks to Reverend Aubrey Keys, who mentored me through the publishing process, and Dr. Johnny Ray Youngblood and the Saint Paul Community Baptist Church, who put up with my preaching.

INTRODUCTION

I t is safe to say that without The Cross, there is no Christianity. The Cross of Jesus has served as the pivotal experience whereby we truly come to understand the depth of God's love. It is The Cross on which Jesus was crucified that we begin to understand the extreme measures that God will go to redeem us. The Cross, within the Christian faith, has evolved from being an instrument of cruelty used by the Romans to discourage rebellion to becoming a symbol of sacred significance. It is such an intricate symbol of the Christian faith that we can hardly imagine Christianity without it.

The songs and litany of The Cross within Christendom give poetic testimony to the indelible impact of what really was a cosmic tragedy. I hold that The Cross was a disaster zone, because of the depth of evil so reprehensibly therein revealed. The world paused on September 11, 2002, to commemorate one of the most heinous acts of terror inflicted upon America. A year earlier, four passenger planes were commandeered by a fanatical faction of religious people and used as deadly missiles for the death of nearly three thousand people and the destruction of billions of dollars in capitol. Where once stood a towering complex known as the World Trade Center, we now have a deep chasm known as Ground Zero. A complex web of socioeconomic realities,

> "THE CROSS HAS UNUSUAL MEANING FOR AFRICAN AMERICANS BECAUSE OF A HISTORY SHAPED BY A LEGACY OF SLAVERY AND RELENTLESS RACISM."

combined with religious fanaticism, produced yet another awful episode of human evil. The world literally changed on September 11, 2001 as the result of a disaster.

The Cross was the Ground Zero of the Christian church. It revealed just how bad we can treat one another. At The Cross we come face-to-face with the intensity that evil human beings can inflict upon one another. Everything evil and awful about humanity was revealed on the Cross.

The Cross has unusual meaning for African Americans, who have a special affinity with it because of a history shaped by a legacy of slavery and relentless racism. The experience of chattel slavery and a continuing struggle against the harsh currents of racism has clearly acquainted African Americans with the horrors of human evil. The drama of chattel slavery and the consequent loss of millions of lives, along with the terrorist trauma inflicted by an obstinately racist civilization, has produced a Ground Zero like chasm within the soul of African people everywhere. African American people know what it means to live out a cross experience because we are painfully acquainted with the horrors of human evil. Such an affinity with human evil moved African Americans to raise up in song, the question: "Were you there when they crucified my Lord?"

Although the Cross does not have the last word about God's intent on human redemption; it does have a vital word, and, indeed, a defining word. It is not just something for us to sing and preach about. The Cross, ironically, also serves as a vital paradigm for ministry within the African American community. It provides a powerfully Christ-centered perspective by which meaningful ministry can be shaped.

The African American church has been able to use the scene of The Cross to catch glimpses of redemptive possibilities. The redemptive purposes of God, as revealed at The Cross, have inspired the African American church to consider life-transforming ministry in the disaster areas of urban America, communities often ravaged by the savage greed of corporate America and the insensitivity of white politicians. A community without healthy social support has too often bred a deep sense of communal despair that becomes painfully self-destructive. It has been in these kinds of contexts where visionary African American church leadership has dared to see Jesus.

> "INTRINSIC TO THE SEVEN SAYINGS ARE POWERFUL POSSIBILITIES BY WHICH CHRISTIANS ARE ABLE TO VIEW THE WORLD AND GIVE MEANING TO THEIR OWN SUFFERING."

I believe that The Cross of Jesus provides a paradigmatic image by which the Saint Paul Community Baptist Church in Brooklyn, New York, has engaged in ministry in the last twenty-five years. Although the church's mantra is "Living in the Power of the Resurrected Lord," the sobering influence of The Cross resonates powerfully in the background. The suffering of The Cross gives shape to the celebration of the resurrection. All who have ever seriously served in the African American church know that there is no crown without a cross.

Under the leadership of Reverend Dr. Johnny Ray Youngblood, the Saint Paul Community Baptist Church has engaged in life-changing ministry in a community that was literally a disaster zone. Even as he struggles to diminish the symbol of The Cross as the definitive Christian symbol, this dynamic and visionary leader has led a congregation to impact a ravaged community in an unprecedented manner. Reverend Youngblood has looked upon the ruins of a crucified community and brought forth redemptive realities.

For the last nine years, I have been privileged to serve in the borough of Brooklyn with Pastor Youngblood. During those nine years, I have been blessed to preach in a gala experience known within the African American church community as the "Seven Last Words". The Seven Last Words are strangely neither seven words nor the last words of Jesus. They are actually seven sayings that are traditionally held to have been uttered from The Cross. During the crucifixion of Jesus, as he was hanging on The Cross, these seven saying were to have fallen from his lips. In each of the sayings, Christians believe essential truths about the meaning of Jesus, as well as the good news implicit in His suffering. Intrinsic to the seven sayings are powerful possibilities by which Christians are able to view the world and give meaning to their own suffering.

It should be noted that African American Christians do not generally promote The Cross as an invitation to suffering, but it is clearly the acknowledgement of suffering particularly among the oppressed. As an interpreter of the Christian faith within the African American

community, I have considered the so-called
Seven Last Words of Jesus as providing
powerful speech by which oppressed people
can articulate redemptive suffering. It is from
the perspective of redemption that the Seven
Last Words of Jesus have been held in high
regard within the African American community.
The observance of the Seven Last Words of
Jesus takes place on Good Friday, usually
with seven different preachers sharing the
preaching responsibilities. The celebration
is in a form of worship often extending to
three hours in length. In recent years other
forms of creative pageantry have been added
to the worship experience, yet the preaching
experience remains an anticipatory mainstay.
Regrettably many of the preaching experiences
around the Seven Last Words have become
thoughtless and unchallenging, or opportunities
for preaching theatrics. In many instances,
the goal of using each of the sayings of our
Lord for liberating admonishments have been
minimized by preaching trivialities.

Although I serve in a different section of
Brooklyn with some slightly different social
maladies, I have been blessed to preach at
Saint Paul Community Baptist Church for the
Seven Last Words experience. During this
experience, I have been challenged to not
approach the task as an opportunity to engage
in lighthearted homilies nor to participate in

a preaching contest. I have tried to approach it as a humble opportunity to speak to a special group of people who have dared to do something concrete about the social maladies of a depressed community. I have asked God to allow me to preach a word that would help the people who dared to serve in a context left to languish in the despair of socio-economic crucifixion. Thus, my preaching efforts have tried to bring The Cross of Jesus to bear upon the contextual realities of this special community.

What has made this task such a joy is the tremendous level of receptivity created by the twenty-five years of bold preachments by Reverend Youngblood. His sermonic creativity and bold prophetic utterances plowed for me a fertile opportunity to preach on another level. I know of no other church community where the humble efforts of any preacher are so joyfully received and appreciated. A preacher burdened with pastoral woes and sermonic doubts can be greatly inspired by the receptive witness of Saint Paul Community Baptist Church.

In the past eight years I have also been privileged to be the only preacher who has been invited each of the last eight years to preach in the Seven Last Words at Saint Paul. It has been my joyful task to preach all seven of the Last Words of Jesus, and the Seventh Word twice, all of which I include here.

Needless to say, one of my constant struggles was to locate relevant resources that would be sensitive to the issues facing the African American community. Needless to say, such resources were not available. The available resources lacked relevant insights critical to people who do ministry within the disaster zones of urban America.

It is my hope that this collection of sermons will in some way contribute toward filling the aching void I faced. As a pastor of a church in urban America, I know what it means to try and preach a relevant word while ministering in a disaster zone. The exegetical fodder of white academicians falls painfully short when a preacher needs a word for the brothers and sisters. I also hope that the printed text of my sermonic struggles on the Seven Last Words will enrich the faith of the faithful parishioners who remain faithful to the African American churches that yet remain in urban America. Hence, I offer upon the altar of hermeneutical sacrifice a preaching perspective of The Cross. It may come off as foolishness to the wise, but for those being saved, it is the power of God.

I was taught that a text without a context is a pretext. In other words, what we say ought to reflect what we know to be true about when it was said, or we mislead people. The wisdom of these words ought to reach beyond our interpretation of scripture. We ought to see

the wisdom of these words influencing even
the contexts of our presentation. What we
say ought to have something to say about the
social context of the people we are saying it to.
(Samuel G. Freedman's book, Upon This Rock:
The Miracles of a Black Church, provides an
incredibly powerful treatment of the Saint Paul
Community Baptist Church, as well as Pastor
Youngblood.) This is must reading for all who
would be inspired to do ministry in urban
America. One statement written by Freedman
provides a glimpse of the urban setting in
which God placed Reverend Youngblood and
the Saint Paul Community Baptist Church:

"From the time his church moved onto
Hendrix Street that February [1980],
Reverend Youngblood had been bothered
by a particular irony: Saint Paul Community
Baptist Church could call nothing in the
surrounding community its own. If anything,
the congregation was held hostage and its
religious values mocked by what happened
along Stanley Avenue. Purses were snatched,
chains ripped from necks, car batteries stolen.
The few legitimate stores struggled amid the
fried-chicken joint that ran numbers, the social
club that sold drugs, the boutique that offered
both, the market that short-weighted old meat.
One local character collected boxes of garbage
at the corner of Stanley and Hendrix and
stacked them into a kind of neighborhood urinal

so foul no carter
would consent
to remove it.
The breaking
point came the
day a competitor
set fire to
the numbers
spot as nearly
one thousand

"GOD WILL SPEAK
THROUGH US TO
SPEAK TO US."

worshiped in Saint Paul, easily within range of
a spreading blaze."[1]

To further your appreciation of the
context of these messages I have included
in the appendix an abbreviated history of the
Saint Paul Community Baptist Church under
the leadership of Reverend Youngblood. An
understanding of the context provides keen
insight into the intention of the following
messages. As there is no understanding of
Good Friday without the explanation provided
on Resurrection Sunday, I have also included
in the prologue a Resurrection response,
which is also expressed sermonically in a
sermon entitled, "Resurrection in the Home."
This sermon was inspired by the preaching
experience of the Seven Last Words at Saint
Paul. It is with a deep sense of pride that I
present these sermons as preached at the Saint
Paul Community Baptist Church.

In revisiting these sermons, I was

profoundly impacted by the divine irony of
the preaching experience. This notion kept
showing up as I became reintroduced to what
I had said during the preaching experiences.
Over and over again as I read I had to ask
myself, "Did I say that?" There were repeated
instances where what I said then spoke directly
to my continuing struggles to live a life of faith
now. In every word, God brought something to
my attention that applied to me, and much of
it had current application. The divine irony of
preaching suggests that God will speak through
us to speak to us. The sermons we preach are
probably as much for us as they are for those
to whom we preach. The matter of the Word
being a "two-edged sword" was powerfully
evident as God used His Word to cut through
the marrow of my own spirit. God was literally
speaking to me as He was speaking through
me. It may be a good idea for us, preachers, to
occasionally revisit our sermons and see what
God is saying to us as God speaks through us.
Nonetheless, I offer these sermonic struggles
as my homiletical reactions to the Christian's
Ground Zero – Calvary.

1
THE FIRST WORD:

A Faith for Bad-Acting People

"And when they had come to the place called Calvary, there they crucified Him, and the criminals, one on the right hand, and the other on the left. Then Jesus said, 'Father, forgive them, for they do not know what they do' And they divided His garments and cast lots." (Luke 23:33-34)

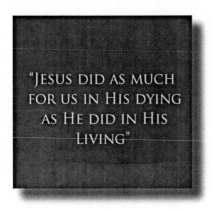

"JESUS DID AS MUCH FOR US IN HIS DYING AS HE DID IN HIS LIVING"

We are here to again consider Jesus' words from Calvary. As I was pondering over Christ's words from the Cross, God revealed to me that God can use our words in ways far more powerful than in our well-prepared, structured sermons. Further revealed to me was that this first word just ought to be the First Word. The First Word reveals to us that Jesus did as much for us in His dying as He did in His living. In fact, there is enough religion in the First Word to radically change our entire world. Our lives can be revolutionized by any sincere effort to embrace the First Word.

Considering the fact that Jesus' life centered around restoring people into harmony with divine intention implies that His First Word ought to, indeed, reflect what His life was all about. His life was primarily about reconciliation, therefore, His death ought to address reconciliation first. We don't find any contradiction in Jesus' death and His dying. What He lived about, He died doing. I hold that Jesus' First Word from the Cross provides us the faith parameters for dealing with life's bad-acting people.

If you have been on this planet for a few days, you would have already concluded that our world has a generous portion of bad-acting people. Bad-acting people are alive and well and active in every area of life. We have bad-acting parents, bad-acting children, bad-acting wives, bad-acting husbands, bad-acting family members, bad-acting employers, bad-acting employees, bad-acting fellow workers, bad-acting businesspeople, bad-acting politicians. The tragedy of Abner Louima and Amadou Diallo clearly remind us that we have some bad-acting police.[2]

We have some bad-acting lawyers, bad-acting bankers, bad-acting teachers, bad-acting neighbors, bad-acting church folk, and even some bad-acting preachers. It does not matter the station in life, there are some bad-acting people in our world! Thus, what I hear coming from the First Word of Jesus is a faith perspective for living with bad-acting people.

The reason this message is so important is because without such a faith perspective, bad-acting people have the potential to produce and perpetuate some more bad-acting people. Jesus' First Word represents God's way of reducing the population of bad-acting people. Without the faith of Jesus as expressed in this First Word, the noblest possibilities of human relationships are severely undermined. We need this First Word to diminish the power of bad-acting people.

To understand the significance of the First Word, it may be helpful for us to consider what The Cross represents. It represents the place where the depths of human evil came out in the open. Jesus's crucifixion reveals just how awful people can be to others. The horrors of human evil show their collective hand at the Cross. One writer said, "The Cross is the symbol, alive and vivid, of the evil that is in us, of the evil itself." It reveals as much about the "crucifiers" as it does about the One being crucified. The evil that is potentially within all of us shows up at The Cross. It lets us see that in any given situation, the best people can become bad-acting. There is within the best of us the worst of us.

Jesus was crucified by an intense demonstration of human evil. The reason Jesus can save to the utmost is because He suffered at the hand of our utmost evil. Listen to Jesus's words!

There within the grasp of horrifying evil, severe injustice, He turned the attention from Himself to others. Of all the many things He could have said, He said, "Father, forgive them!" He was being grossly mistreated. He could have said, "Avenge me! Send forth a legion of angels and strike these bad-acting people." He could have said, "Rescue me! Do whatever You need to do to get me out of this humiliating fix." He could have said, "Justify me! Do whatever it takes to prove to these people that I am right and they are wrong." He could have at least said, "Comfort me. Please do something to anesthetize the pain." (Some of us can surely think of some other choice things He could have said.) Of the many things He could have said, Jesus said, "Forgive them!"

This may well be the most saving word of our faith. All of us, who really know God know Him because He has forgiven us. If our world is to ever recover from its hell-bent posture, forgiveness will have to become a reality. We have a city administration that suggested changing bullets and then changing the uniforms, will correct the bad-behavior of bad-acting police. People don't stop being bad just because they change clothes. Taking off a hood and putting on a suit doesn't stop a person from being a racist. If America is to ever be healed from the evils of racism, sexism, imperialism, egoism, consumerism, militarism, jingoism, and all of its many relationship-shattering evils forgiveness will have to become a reality.

When Jesus said, "forgive them," He was literally asking God to remove all evidence of the evil that keeps people out of relationship with God, self, and others. "Forgive them! Take

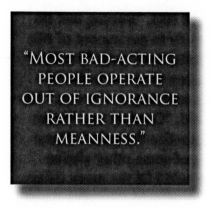

"MOST BAD-ACTING PEOPLE OPERATE OUT OF IGNORANCE RATHER THAN MEANNESS."

away whatever it is that hinders people from engaging in wholesome respectful relationships. Forgive them! Extract from their midst that which hurts them the most. Forgive them! Take away the impediments to a wholesome relationship with God." Forgiveness has to be the First Word, or all the other words wouldn't mean anything. "Forgive them!"

Here is the only word that provides a faith perspective for bad-acting people. Some of you have come here today with lives troubled by bad-acting people. They are in our homes, on our jobs, at schools, on our block, in our city hall, and even in our churches. How can we appropriate a faith perspective for bad-acting people?

Have you ever considered that one of the most wonderful features of an automobile is reverse? Reverse puts a vehicle in a place where going forward is useless. What could we ever do with a car that never backed up? I took the liberty to use a hermeneutical reverse and backed into this text in order to extrapolate the essence of a faith for bad-acting people. And

since we are going to have to live with bad-
acting people for the rest of our lives, even the
bad actor within, a reverse hermeneutic can
take us where going forward would fail.

It would help our faith perspective to know,
as did Jesus, that most bad-acting people
operate out of ignorance rather than meanness.
Jesus noted that the cause for all of this bad-
acting behavior is because "they know not
what they do." They are not necessarily mean.
They are afflicted with a bad case of the "don't
knows." Ignorance can turn good-acting people
into bad-acting people. Ignorance, mind you,
is not the lack of knowledge. Unintelligent
people could never have crucified Jesus.
Intelligent people crucified Jesus. The truth
is a lot of highly intelligent people can be
severely ignorant, and people who never attend
school and are not certified by the culture
can be extremely wise. Ignorance is a choice,
whereas meanness is a disposition. Ignorance
is choosing to ignore the truth.

Jesus said, "I am the way, the truth, and the
life."[3] He also said, "You shall know the truth
and the truth shall make you free."[4] Whenever
people choose to ignore the truth, they become
prime candidates for becoming bad-acting
people. People who choose to ignore the truth
will hurt others. People who become what
my friend, Reverend Manuel Scott, Jr. called
"truth fugitives" will kill someone. Blacks have

a history of being hurt because white people choose to ignore the truth that all people are created equal. Men have hurt women because men choose to ignore the truth that women are just as skillful as men. That is just the truth!

Some of this pain we are enduring, and some of this guilt we are bearing could be healed by several large doses of truth. Moreover, we can more redemptively deal with bad-acting people when we realize they are not functioning out of meanness, but out of ignorance. When we know that people are ignoring the truth, we don't feel the need to retaliate, and we can be more compassionate. We have no desire to hurt people for their bad-acting behavior. We can have the compassion of Jesus who said, "Forgive them, for they know not what they do." We can better love people when we understand their condition. We can avail ourselves to serve others, even when we know that they might hurt us, for they don't know what they do. They are not mean they are ignorant.

Luke tells us that Jesus was crucified between two thieves. He was placed between two socially recognized bad actors, yet, if we look closer at the text, we see Luke including a crowd of socially acceptable folk who were worst than the criminals. Luke says, "When they came to the place called the Skull, there they crucified him." Verse 34 adds, "And they divided up his clothes."

Second, a faith perspective for living with bad-acting people understands that in every bad-acting deed, there is plurality not just individuality. Jesus understood that sin is a group thing. My homiletical professor, David Buttrick, noted, "as an individual we may struggle with inner dispositions, but as a group we become deadly." Jesus pluralized the "crucifiers" for all crucifiers function out of a network of crowds.

People who do evil to others most often act out of the deviance of crowds. People who act badly rarely act alone. Bad-acting people represent social patterns and have a history of playing out certain scripts that have been handed down through time. Like the Gadarenes mad man,[5] claimed to have represented a community of devils, bad-acting people tend to have a bad-acting ancestry.

Look at the crowd at Jesus' crucifixion! It appears that every arena of society was represented. Pilate and Herod represented the politicians. Although Pilate found no fault, he didn't do what he could have done to prevent the crucifixion. Political expediency has a tendency to do innocent people a lot of harm.

The legal system, Pharisees and Sadducees sponsored a kangaroo court. Jesus didn't have O. J. Simpson's money, so he was railroaded through the system. He was lynched by a legal system that had a history of doing some cruel things. Legal bad actors gave legal sanction to the crucifixion.

Jesus' friends, along with the infamous Judas, forsook and betrayed Him. Close associates can sometimes be your worst enemies. The disciples were as faithless as Judas was ruthless. Faithlessness can be just as injurious as ruthlessness.

The Roman soldiers represented the evils of militarism. The thoughtless obedience to orders can turn good people into bad-acting people. Whoever produced the wood used to construct the Cross represented the business world. Someone either sold or donated the wood served at the Cross. We can do some terrible things in the name of good business. Business has an awful record of producing bad-acting people. Slavery was big business. Prostitution, the exploitation of women for the pleasure of men is big business. Drug trafficking, the illegal contracts of drugs used to destroy the lives of oppressed people is big business. Child pornography is big business. There just ought to be some things we won't do for money.

There was the sadistic crowd cheering, "Crucify him, crucify him!" Violence as entertainment has long history. The people spat upon him. They mocked him, "If you can save others save yourself." The tendency of people to join in with the herd can turn good people into bad-acting ones. I've witnessed good Christians join in with the crowd and do some terrible things.

> "ONLY A VIEW OF THE COLLECTIVE MADNESS WITHIN US ALL CAN EMPOWER US TO FORGIVE ONE ANOTHER."

Religion was there. The High Priest, Caiaphas, and Annas were there with all the supporters of organized religion. Caiaphas, the moderator, convention president, and denominational official, led the crowd in this dastardly deed. Organized religion can become so self-serving that we produce bad-acting people. We can't adequately explain Henry J. Lyons[6] without including the inadequacies of organized religion. Lyons may go to jail, but all of these self-serving conventions need to repent and confess that we are all a company of bad actors.

Only a view of the collective madness within us all can empower us to forgive one another. Forgiveness is essentially an act of liberation. Jesus sets people free from the evils of crowds and social patterns. Only the liberated can discern that the evils people do are the result of a plurality, and not just an individuality.

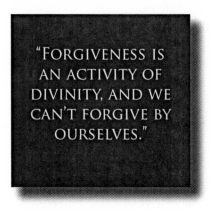

"FORGIVENESS IS AN ACTIVITY OF DIVINITY, AND WE CAN'T FORGIVE BY OURSELVES."

I mentioned earlier that I used a reverse hermeneutic and backed into this text. This was necessary because the first word of Jesus's First Word represented His most powerful Word. If I had started with this first word of the First Word, I wouldn't have had much else to say. Notice, Jesus's First Word never referred to Himself. His attention went away from Himself and turned to others. Yet, the first word of the First Word was Father.

Jesus operated from a faith perspective that believed divine intervention would erase evil intention. Whatever evil people do to us, God can remove the evil from us. Once we embrace the love of God, we do not have to tote the luggage of an unforgiving spirit. Joseph understood this principle when he told his brothers, "You meant it for evil, but God meant it for good."[7]

Brothers and sisters, Jesus helps us to see that there are some things we can't do by ourselves. Forgiveness is an activity of divinity, and we can't forgive by ourselves. Jesus did not tell the people, "I forgive you." He asked God to forgive them. Jesus understood that if God forgave them, He would have to forgive them. Only God has the power to ratify forgiveness. When we come to really know God, we know that He is a forgiving God. I have heard people say, "There are some things I can never forgive a person for." The truth is that bad-acting people do hurt us to the point that we can never forgive them on our own power. Yes, there are some evils we suffer where our efforts of forgiveness are inadequate.

When I first drove into New York, I had a car that had an electronic transmission. It had regular gears: park, neutral, drive, drive one and drive two. But, it also had a "super" gear. I rarely used the super gear because with ordinary driving the regular gears were adequate; however, there were some times when the regular gears were inadequate and I had to switch to super. Whenever I switched to super the car would jump forth with neck-breaking power.

Brothers and sisters that is what Jesus did with the First Word. That is what Jesus did at the place called the Skull. When faced with such a mass of bad actors, Jesus switched to "Father Power." In doing so, Jesus helped us to see that when we are faced with bad-acting people, it is best to shift to Father Power. There are some people who we must deal with on the divine thrust of Father Power. Since we all know that God forgives us, we also must know that God forgives bad-acting people.

When people are deceitful and devilish, switch to Father Power.

When people are immoral and perverted, switch to Father Power.

When people act selfish and sinful, switch to Father Power.

When people are vulgar and vile, switch to Father Power.

When people are violent and mean, switch to Father Power.

When people are indifferent and insensitive, switch to Father Power.

When this world lets you know that it is no friend to grace, switch to Father Power. Let us join with the songwriter and say:

Father, I stretch my hands to thee;
No other help I know.
If thou withdraw thyself from me,
Oh, wither shall I go.

2

THE SECOND WORD:

Conversation in a Crisis - Three Words Before the Darkness

"Then one of the criminals who were hanged blasphemed Him, saying, 'If You are the Christ, save Yourself and us.' But the other, answering, rebuked him, saying, 'Do you not even fear God, seeing you are under the same condemnation? And we indeed justly, for we receive the due reward for our deeds; but this Man has done nothing wrong.' Then he said to Jesus, 'Lord, remember me when You come into Your kingdom.' And Jesus said to him, 'Assuredly, I say to you, today you will be with Me in Paradise.'" (Luke 23:39-43)

The second word of Jesus is actually the third word within a three-part conversation. The other words from The Cross on Calvary are basically pronouncements and prayers. This word is couched within a conversation. The second word is the only one from the Cross where Jesus engaged in one of the most unique features of our humanity, which is conversation. At the conclusion of the conversation, in the following verse, Luke 23:44, the Bible says, "And it was about the sixth hour, and there was darkness over all the earth."

I can think of a number of things that make human beings God's most interesting creatures. We have hands that make us the only tool users on the planet. We have imaginations that make us the most complex, creative, and sometimes most disturbed creatures on the planet. We have faces that broadcast our deepest emotions, even when we don't want anyone to know what is going on within us. The world can generally get a snapshot of our inner disposition by looking in our face. We have attitudes that move us to act contrary to our intelligence level. We have egos that move us to excel, exaggerate, and sometimes orchestrate our own destruction. We are the only creatures on the earth who can organize to destroy one another. Moreover, of all the creatures, we have the power of speech that allows us to engage one another in conversation.

"A CRISIS WILL MAKE REAL OUR CONVERSATION."

We are creatures of conversation. We talk. We engage one another. We communicate thoughts, ideas, information, and feelings. Of interest is the word conversation. Conversation comes from two words that literally mean social intercourse. We exchange our social perspectives through conversation. We don't all exchange the same level of conversation, but all of us are creatures of conversation.

As I listened in on the conversation between the two criminals and the Christ, it came to me that what's really inside of us comes out when in a crisis. We speak our true selves in a crisis. We really show the world what we are when in trouble or when life-threatening difficulty comes onto our lives. As a people, we have been conditioned to exercise controlled speech. In normal circumstances we can exchange ideas, thoughts, and information that have nothing to do with anything; however, let the situation change or put our lives at risk and that is when what's inside of us really comes out. A crisis will make real our conversation.

We all have to believe that Calvary was a crisis situation. It was not only a crisis between the will of evil and the will of God, but it was a crisis for all who experience crucifixion. There at the place of the Skull, all who threatened the might of Rome were impaled on wood to discourage any notion of insurrection. Rome called the crucifixion, tokens of punishment, a form of punishment borrowed from the Carthaginians. It was a form of punishment normally reserved for slaves, or for those who were oppressed.

Unlike the cute Jesus we profile on our gold and silver crosses, Rome impaled suspected insurrectionists in the most grotesque manner possible to promote shame, degradation, and humiliation. Two known criminals and the Christ shared in this barbaric form of punishment. There was nothing cute about it, and it was not intended for religious purposes. They were experiencing the most painful, life-threatening experience of their existence. They were being crucified.

They were in a crisis. They were in the epicenter of salvation's Ground Zero. (In the Third Word, I refer to it as a disaster zone.) They were at a place that if ideas, thoughts, and information were to be exchanged, it would reveal what was really inside of them. They were at a place where if there were social intercourse, there would be no need for the prophylactics of idle talk. This was a time to get to the real. Cut to the chase! It was time to speak from a place of death and dying and announce what was really inside of them.

As we eavesdrop on the conversation in a crisis, three words from three different people are clearly heard. Three words from different directions and different perspectives are uttered. The name of one person is widely known. His name is even stated in the text. The other two men's names were not so commonly known, but I checked the Jerusalem Globe and discovered their names were Joathas and Maggatras. The second criminal was also known as Dsymas.

The first criminal, Joathas, spoke a word of resentment. As the darkness was creeping upon the earth, he said, "If you are the Christ, save Yourself and us." His word is a word of resentment. His word is a word intended to hurt, filled with sick indignation. He literally joined in with the sneering and mocking of the rulers and soldiers and blasphemed the Lord. "If you are the Christ, save Yourself and us." His voice rings with the satanic jeer of the temptations, "If you be the Christ."[8] What makes him sound so much like a "brotha" is what he added. He added "and us." Like some ancient Jamie Foxx or first century

Steve Harvey, "If you do get yourself out of this tight, don't forget about us." His words rang with displeasure. His words echo those of someone who has been so poisoned by oppression that he held anyone who looked like him in the same situation as himself, or going through what he was going through as an object of contempt.

It doesn't take much imagination to hear that word in many of us who have been so poisoned by the toxins of racism and oppression that when it comes to relating with one another, we sound just like the oppressor. We act as if we don't realize that we are in the same boat, suffering the same pains, and dying the same awful death. We "diss" one another. We put down one another. We mock one another. We hear it in our homes. We hear it in our schools. We hear it in the young and the old. We hear it in the music of the hip-hop generation, and we even hear it in the pews and pulpits of the church. A lot of the social intercourse between brothers and sisters is resentment, words that are intended to hurt and ultimately deny our common suffering.

What a terrible word as the darkness comes! What a nasty way of talking to your brother or your sister! Just because your plan to get over fell through, why project toxins of oppression upon another who is feeling what you are feeling, going through whatever you are going through, and who is suffering just like you?

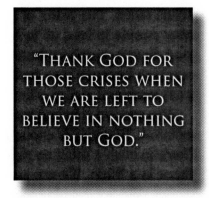

"THANK GOD FOR THOSE CRISES WHEN WE ARE LEFT TO BELIEVE IN NOTHING BUT GOD."

The First Word before the darkness is one of resentment, a toxic and oppressive word. The second word is one of repentance. The second criminal, Maggatras, rebuked his brother in crime. He said, "Do you not even fear God, seeing you are under the same condemnation? And we indeed justly, for we receive the due reward of our deeds; but this man has done nothing wrong." As the darkness crept closer, the second criminal broke rank. He declared liberation from the toxic influences of his crime dog. He seemed to have gone back to his early upbringing, when Momma and Daddy, Big Momma and Big Daddy brought him to church and tried to lead him to an understanding of God. He didn't hear them then, but he sure heard them at that moment.

I thank God for those crises when we are left to believe in nothing but God. God has a way of arranging life that we are left with no one but Him. One thing this brother does that more people, including Christians, need to do, is to know when it is time to break rank and switch sides. Too many of us are allowing other people to lead us to hell. I've watched good church members become bad church members because they lacked the backbone to break rank and switch sides.

The second criminal broke rank and declared, "Enough is enough! There is a God. There is such a thing as right and wrong. There is a Bible. We are getting what we had coming. We are reaping what we have sowed, but this man has done nothing wrong. I know he has done nothing wrong, because I know all the wrongdoers in Jerusalem, and he is not one of them."

Notice his next move. He went all the way. He said, "Lord, remember me when You come into Your kingdom." He seemed to have seen something in Jesus that he had never seen in anyone. He saw a power in Jesus, and he wanted a part in Jesus, even from a cross. He saw that not even a cross was going to negate what Jesus was all about. He asked that Jesus would allow him a chance to participate in the new arrangement of the world. He wanted a place in the Lord's kingdom.

When the darkness comes, a word of repentance is in order. The darkness is looming over some of our lives right now and this word can change our destiny. Some of us need to break rank and cry out to the Lord. Some of us need to change, break rank, and cry out to the Lord. Some of us are in situations where our own power has proven inadequate, our plans have failed, and we now feel impaled upon

"THE LORD WILL ALWAYS GIVE US MORE THAN WE ASK FOR."

the pain of our circumstances. This word says that as the darkness comes we need to change, break rank, switch sides, and cry out to the Lord. "Lord remember me when You come into Your kingdom."

Years ago while at Bishop College, the late Dr. Joseph H. Jackson, who at that time was the immediate past president of the National Baptist Convention, USA, Inc., preached. I was but a student at the time. I was in awe at all the great preachers and leaders in attendance; however, I shall never forget Dr. Jackson's words. He lifted up the gruesome scene at Calvary and declared that the only saving word came from the man in the middle. He noted that the others were but two criminals, common hoodlums, being executed for crimes they even confessed, but the man in the middle was the Savior of the world.

Listen to this last word before the darkness, which comes from Jesus. Jesus answered the criminal, "Assuredly, I say to you today you will be with me in Paradise." Notice, the man asked to be remembered when Jesus came into his kingdom. Jesus said, "Today you will be with me in Paradise." The man asked, "When?" Jesus answered, "Today." The man said, "Kingdom." Jesus answered "Paradise."

The dying man wanted to be thought of when the social order was rearranged and the oppressed would rule the land. He wanted to be a part of a coming social order, a future eschatology; however, I dare anyone to get serious with the Lord. All who get truly serious with Him about seeking new direction in their lives, the Lord will always give us more than we ask for. All who ever get serious and cry out to the Lord know that God always answers with more than we expected. The Bible says, "Eye has not seen, ear has not heard, nor has it entered into the hearts of men what God has in store for those who love him and are called according to his purposes."[9]

The man asked to be remembered in the kingdom. Jesus placed him instantly in paradise. The kingdom is about the rule of God. Paradise is about being in relationship with God. The kingdom is about established order. Paradise is about restored relationships. The kingdom is about right government. Paradise is about right relationships. Jesus was telling the dying man that if you get in the right

relationship, you receive power. If you get
in the right relationship you receive order. If
you get in the right relationship with God, you
come under the rule of God. If you get in the
right relationship, you get all the benefits of the
kingdom.

The dying man asked, "When?" Jesus said,
"Today." Today meant right then. Notice,
brothers and sisters, Jesus said, "Today you
will be with me." I want to know on this Good
Friday, is there anyone willing to be with Jesus
today?

Today, in His suffering.

Today, in His pain.

Today, in His agony.

Today, in His abandonment.

Today, in His dying.

Before the darkness comes, is there anyone
here who wants to be with Jesus today? No
wonder the apostle wrote, I share with Him in
his dying, so that I may share with Him in His
rising. "That I might know Him and the power
of His resurrection, and the fellowship of His
sufferings, being conformed to His death, if
by any means, I may attain to the resurrection
from the dead."[10] Hallelujah! Praise His name!

3

THE THIRD WORD:

Ministry in a Disaster Zone

"Now there stood by the cross of Jesus His mother, and His mother's sister, Mary the wife of Clopas, and Mary Magdalene. When Jesus therefore saw His mother, and the disciple whom He loved standing by, He said to His mother, 'Woman, behold your son!' Then he said to the disciple, 'Behold your mother.' And from that hour forth that disciple took her to his own home." (John 19:25-27).

> "THE CHURCH OUGHT TO BE DOING ALL IT CAN TO LEAVE THE WORLD BETTER THAN WE FOUND IT."

Some of the most profound statements I have ever read or heard were simple ones. An example of such was made two years ago when a participant of this preaching event stood and simply said, "Jesus had a bad day." A simple statement, yet it echoes with resounding profundity. A friend betrayed Him. Disciples deserted Him. The crowd flip-flopped on Him. Pilate went wimp on Him. The courts went south on Him. Justice went bankrupt on Him. The pain of a crucifixion was inflicted upon Him. Soldiers went bad on Him. The sun went dark on Him. The earth went drunk on Him, and even God took leave on Him. Yes, Jesus had a bad day, and the world experienced a disaster.

My college president, Dr. Harry S. Wright, who now serves as pastor of Cornerstone Baptist Church in Brooklyn, New York, admonished us students at Bishop College to leave the world a little better than we found it. Dr. Wright's words may well be the most focused ones for doing ministry in the new millennium. The church ought to be doing all

it can to leave the world better than we found
it. Of all the great things Jesus did during His
ministry, He did more in His dying than most
do in living. In the midst of a major disaster
Jesus provided for us the most redemptive
model of doing ministry in our respective
disaster zones.

His First Word was directed to His
enemies. While a victim of murder He extended
forgiveness. His Second Word was an offering
of paradise for all who have been designated
as society's excuse for evil in the world. He
would later cry out to God as He agonized
over being forsaken. He cried out for some
expression of compassion from a world that
was no friend to grace.

Of all the words Jesus uttered, this is the
only one addressed exclusively to the church.
Jesus focused the church upon its central
function in a world where people can do some
awful things to other people: do ministry! In
the midst of a horrifying scene where the best
One for us comes in contact with the worst
thing within us, Jesus had but one word for the
church: do ministry! In a world landscaped with
disaster zones, we are called to leave it a little
better than we found it. While we struggle with
our own personal, social, emotional, and even
spiritual disasters, we are called to do ministry.

I have yet to understand why the best thing
we have been able to do with this word is to

glorify motherhood. It is as if we, preachers, believe that this disaster at Calvary took place for us to preach Mother's Day sermons on Good Friday. Motherhood ought to be celebrated, but the scene on The Cross lifts up the horrifying things that happen when people allow evil to dominate their spirits. At The Cross, great and enormous evil took control of the spirits of so-called good people, who revealed the capacity of so-called goodness doing some awful things. The participants in the crucifixion allow us to see the worst in the best of us. Our noblest humanity became the stage prop of a major disaster.

I know we have some good people here, today, but may we never forget that whenever and wherever evil controls the human spirit, we are in a disaster zone. I don't know how you may have interpreted this Elian Gonzalez fiasco.[11] In the midst of it being total nonsense, I am afraid that the evil of American imperialism is being played out in the psyche of a little boy who needs to take his little "behind" home with his father. America will use a six-year-old Cuban boy who it really does not care about just to be right. Also, our mayor has not learned that anyone who clings to a sense of self-righteousness while evil is being inflicted upon people is a walking disaster. "Right" does not mean a thing if people are being abused.

It does not matter how high we shout and

how joyful our noise, it does not erase the fact that most of our churches are located in urban disaster zones. We can never anesthetize ourselves with religious opiates from what is happening within our communities.

Let's be real! We live in the midst of disasters. The black family has become a disaster. We are marrying for the wrong reasons and divorcing twice as fast because of relationship disasters. Single parents are raising most of our children. Grandmothers are being forced to raise the children of their too-high, too-spaced-out, and too-trifling sons and daughters. Call it what you will, it is a disaster!

We still struggle to make it week to week, paycheck to paycheck. With all the black people in New York, we don't own one supermarket, yet we eat up all Waldbaums and Pathmark can sack up. A New York Times editorial suggested that drug dealers are the worst Uncle Toms within the history of African American people. Drug dealers are selling out the black community, while the money is being laundered by corporate America. Too many young black men are satisfied with having high-priced, motorized entertainment centers, which they can park outside of the projects. What a disaster! A major economic boycott will occur when black folk simply say, "We ain't getting high anymore."

Just as Jesus did ministry in a disaster zone,

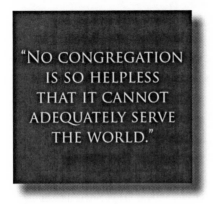

"NO CONGREGATION IS SO HELPLESS THAT IT CANNOT ADEQUATELY SERVE THE WORLD."

the black church is being called to do ministry in disaster zones. We have been blessed to have more churches in Brooklyn than we have liquor stores. We have churches on top of churches, but when the church fails to do ministry it is not a mere oversight. It is blatant disobedience. And to disobey God is a major disaster. In other words, when the church fails to do ministry while in the midst of human disasters, the church itself becomes a disaster.

It does not matter what we do, if our major premise is to disobey God and do what we want to do, we engage in disastrous activities. To not be a praying people is to invite disaster. To neglect tithing is to commit suicide of the soul. To not allow God to use us wherever we are with whatever we have is to lock ourselves into one disaster after another.

What Jesus did on The Cross in this Third Word was to remove all excuses for not doing ministry. We have no excuse. Jesus was having a bad day and did good ministry. He was broke. He had no building and no one following Him. There was no position other than to be hung

high and stretched wide on a rugged cross.
Jesus hung on a Cross and engaged in ministry.
He said, "Woman, behold your son!" Then he
said to the disciple, "Behold your mother!"

As Jesus died for the sins of the world,
He paused long enough to engage the church
in ministry to the world. Jesus' words to His
mother and friend are words for the church
in the midst of disaster. Jesus helps us to
see that our situations are never too critical
where we cannot do ministry. No church is
so out of it that it cannot engage in ministry.
No congregation is so helpless that it cannot
adequately serve the world.

John as gospel of metaphors used the
principle characters involved in this word as
metaphors for doing ministry. The first person
who provides insight on how to do ministry in
a disaster area was Jesus' mother. A mother
informs us that ministry takes risk. The same
mother who took the risk of bringing Jesus
into the world was taking another risk as Jesus
was being destroyed by the world. If there was
anyone who wanted to alleviate the pains of
Jesus, it was His mother. Mothers can't help
but be mothers, even in the midst of disasters.

In the days of Jesus, the key function of
a mother was to be a nurturer. Nurturing
involved giving of one's self for the sake of
another. Jesus was calling for the nurturing
function of Mary to be transferred into the life

of one whose life could be destroyed by the disaster of the Cross. She could do for Jesus by doing for John.

If the church is to be a ministering presence within the disasters of our world, we must become a nurturing presence in the lives of those being overwhelmed by human evil. Like a mother who loves a child for the sake of the child, a nurturing church is one that gives itself for the sake of others. A church that seeks to be served stops being a church. Like a mother who suffers so that the children may live, the church must be willing to suffer so that others may live.

I shall never forget Mother Collier, a faithful member of the Olivet Missionary Baptist Church, my first pastorate. Mother Collier once stood and testified of having starved herself so that her children could eat. She cooked the food, prepared the food, set it on the table and wouldn't eat any.

The children would ask her if she was going to eat. She would lie and say she snacked during its preparation. Her present state of health reflects the trauma of accumulated personal sacrifice. That is the kind of sacrifice made when you are only interested in the welfare of others. Jesus knew that the world needed a nurturing presence, a community of believers who would be concerned about the welfare of others.

One other thing must be said about mother as nurturer. The Bible says, "Jesus saw His mother."[12] In the midst of a disaster, Jesus saw His mother. When all had forsaken Him and the world had crucified Him, Jesus saw His mother. Brothers and sisters, a good nurturer will stand by when no one else will. Such is the kind of church that will make a difference in our communities – one that will stand by people when no one else will. Maybe that is what moved the songwriter to write:

> *At the Cross, at the Cross*
> *Where I first saw the light,*
> *And the burden of my heart rolled away.*
> *It was there by faith*
> *I received my sight,*
> *And now I am happy all the day!*

What a testimony for the church! If the hurting people within Bedford Stuyvesant and East New York could testify, "The church stood by me when no one else did. The church stood by me when all had forsaken me. In the midst of my personal and family disaster, I saw the church when I didn't see anyone else. When my world blew apart and lay in shambles, I was nurtured by the church." Mother, behold your son. Ministry involves providing nurture.

The second person who gives powerful insight on ministering in a disaster zone was

"MINISTRY INVOLVES GIVING A FUTURE."

John. Jesus saw John. Jesus' words to John via Mary were, "Behold your son. Son, behold your mother." The ancient Hebrews regarded a son as critical for the future of a family or community. The oldest son represented the most important person for a family or a community's future. Jesus was Mary's oldest son. Thus, when Jesus was being crucified Mary was witnessing the painful disaster of her family's future. The Cross was a disaster to future possibilities. Jesus' words to His mother served notice that the disaster of The Cross was not canceling out the future. "Woman, behold your son. Son, behold your mother." Ministry involves giving a future.

A young man was recently involved in a very tragic chain of events. A life was lost, a family was destroyed, and his own future was tragically altered. When asked why he did what he did, he could only answer, "I don't know." So much of the disastrous turns taken are often answered with an "I don't know." Lives are being destroyed and young people don't even know the ramifications of their actions. They lack a perspective of the future. The major reason why so many young black females find themselves mothers before their time is because they lack a sense of the future. The frightening return of depressant drug usage, such as heroin, is because so many have given up on the future.

It's rather hard to carve out a future in a world where disasters have become so common. When we look at what is happening today, why plan for tomorrow? This lack of a future has rendered impotent the possibilities of many people. I doubt if anyone can give a definitive picture of black America, yet, this lack of a clear future is not new to the Christian church. Paul once struggled with a church that had lost a sense of future. He replied, "If we have no hope, we are people most miserable." [13]

When the church ministers to people in the midst of disasters, we provide a future. Only the church can direct the eyes of this world beyond the ugliness of Friday to the glory of Sunday. Only the church can declare, "Weeping may endure for a night, but joy comes in the morning." Only the church can peer into the dark of the night and declare, "There is a bright side somewhere."

We are called to stand with those devastated by life's disasters and declare, "Tomorrow will make a difference." We don't always know what tomorrow brings, we only know Who holds tomorrow. Ministering in the name of Jesus serves notice that disasters don't have the last word. To engage in ministry is to recognize that something good can come out of the worst situation. We can be blessed from blunders, and God can make a miracle out of our mess. "All things work together for the good."

The future is one of the primary gifts of ministry. We give a future because we present a Savior, which leads me to the most important person present at Calvary. It took the Savior to set in motion the nurturing function of ministry. It took the Savior to provide the future power of ministry. Jesus saw the disasters of mother and friend and transformed them into ministering delights. They knew, as we should know, that when Jesus tells us to do something, He also promises to be in what we do. Ministry promotes the Savior.

When we minister within the disaster zones of our world, we bring a Savior in the midst of disaster. The Lord promised us in Matthew 28:19-20, that if we go, He will go with us. A Savior is exactly what the name suggests, one who saves. Jesus is the One who saves. What people ultimately need in disasters is One who saves.

I have been in situations where good advice was not good enough. I have had people call on me where my help wasn't helpful enough. I have gone to people's aid, and my aid was not good enough. I have seen people in fixes where nothing I knew would fix the situation. I have witnessed people down in the dumps and nothing seemed to lift them up. I've seen homes so wrecked that counseling could not correct them. I've received calls where hurts were so great that I began to hurt myself. I've had people come to me with tears so plenty that I joined them in crying. I've personally known burdens so great that I was weakened.

Brothers and sisters, the best we can do for people is to introduce them to the One who saves. Jesus saves!

When words are insufficient, there is One who saves.

When advice is inadequate, there is One who saves.

When our help is not helpful, there is One who saves.

When our money can't bail us out, there is One who saves.

When evil overwhelms, there is One who saves.

When a heart is broken, there is One who saves.

When a burden is crushing, there is One who saves.

When tears are gushing, there is One who saves.

When death is rushing, there is One who saves. His name is Jesus. He is the One who saves. Whatever the disaster, join with the songwriter and plead:

Pass me not O gentle Savior
Hear my humble cry.
While on others thou art calling,
Do not pass me by.

THE FOURTH WORD:

Promising Speech From a Painful Place

"Now the sixth hour had come, there was darkness over the whole land until the ninth hour. And at the ninth hour Jesus cried out with a loud voice, saying, 'Eloi, Eloi, lama sabachthani?' Which is translated, 'My God, My God, why have You forsaken Me?'" (Mark 15:33–34)

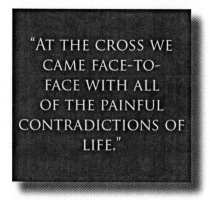

"AT THE CROSS WE CAME FACE-TO-FACE WITH ALL OF THE PAINFUL CONTRADICTIONS OF LIFE."

Inasmuch as the Christian faith is a joyous faith, its joy comes by the way of great pain. One of the many insights on life provided by the Christian faith is that true joy is accompanied by great pain. As we draw near to the day in which we give pronounced celebration to the Resurrection, we must pause and ponder The Cross. Two of our favorite songs are "Jesus, Keep Me Near the Cross," and "At the Cross," yet the truth is that The Cross is a place of great pain.

At The Cross we come face-to-face with all the painful contradictions of life. Jesus was nailed to The Cross. The Cross was the place where evil took a bold stand and launched an ugly assault upon innocence and justice. The Cross was the place where goodness was crucified. The Cross is a symbol of the awful extent evil goes to uphold unjust structures created and sustained by human beings. Whatever seemed unfair about life got an opportunity to express itself at The Cross. However we express our reverence and adoration to The Cross – The Cross was a painful place.

Consider what painful realities unfold at the Cross: The very Son of God was lynched by an angry mob. He was murdered not because of His guilt, but because of His innocence. He was executed not because of anything mischievous, but from everything that was meritorious. He was saluted as King, not with the words of O King, live forever, but with the words, Crucify Him! Instead of kissing His hand, cruel underlings slapped His face. Instead of a scepter of kingly authority, they placed in his hand reeds, symbols of weakness and of one who had no rights worthy of respecting. Instead of being crowned with jewels and gold, He was crowned with piercing thorns. Instead of bowing down and worshipping Him, they scorned Him by stripping Him naked and dressing Him in someone else's clothes. Instead of a royal court at His side, a rusty sword was thrust in His side. Instead of being showered with love and acceptance, He was pummeled and overwhelmed by hate and rejection. No confetti was rained on Him. His body was soiled with His own blood. The Cross was a painful place.

The Book of Mark highlights the pain of the drama on The Cross by adding the fact that "darkness came over the land." Abraham Smith, a New Testament scholar, reminded us that in Mark the people who were supposed

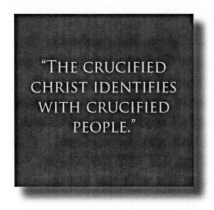

"THE CRUCIFIED CHRIST IDENTIFIES WITH CRUCIFIED PEOPLE."

to know Jesus really didn't know Him. Those who should have understood Him really did not understand Him. Those who should have loved Him really did not love Him. Even on The Cross, Mark does not desert the Messianic secret of Jesus who had been "dropped by His family, refused by His hometown, deserted by His disciples, accused by religious leaders, condemned by the crowds, mocked by soldiers, and taunted by criminals with whom He is executed." And to highlight further the pain of this agonizing place, Mark records Jesus uttering the most heart-rending words of the Bible, "My God, My God, why have You forsaken Me?"

I appreciate the insights of the liberation theologians who understand that the Crucified Christ identifies with the "crucified people." Daily, people are being hung out on crosses of unjust structures and inhuman systems. All over the world, millions are being economically lynched by a system that benefits a few at the expense of the masses. Good Friday continues when forty thousand children under the age of five die every day due to lack of vaccines that prevent childhood diseases, while pharmaceutical companies hold elaborate board meetings to discuss profits. Every day five hundred million people go hungry, while bigger and bigger cruise ships waste more and more food. Over one billion people live in extreme poverty, and over forty million people die yearly of malnutrition and hunger. A Cross has been devised that condemns more than three-fourths of the earth's population to share in only fifteen percent of its resources.

I struggled the other day to explain to my young daughter why a lady under the influence of anesthetics, a yellow phlegm dripping uncontrollably from her mouth, and finger nails with no discernible shape had to stumble into a Chinese restaurant to order some bad food. There was a lady who was a member of the crucified people who had never had a consistent pattern of good nutrition and healthy living conditions. People are being forced to live in some painful places.

I don't know what you believe about Jesus, but I believe that everything He did helps me with life and living. As I listen to him cry out from The Cross, "My God, My God, why have You forsaken Me?" I hear the Crucified Christ providing promising speech for crucified people. I hear Jesus giving language of promise to all those caught in a painful place. I hear

Jesus doing something for you and me that is not always easy to do, that is, to give adequate expression when caught in a painful place. Maybe your situation is good right now, but there comes into the life of every person a period of crucifixion. All of us will have, and some of us have right now, moments of forsakenness. We have those moments when darkness seems to cover the landscape of our lives. The forces of life have an uncanny way of constructing situations and circumstances that are painfully senseless. The people who ought to be with you desert you. Those who can hurt you decide it's time to do so. The economic and political systems have a way of joining in on every crucifixion. And then to make matters worse, all of what we thought we understood about the love of God does not hold up. Yes, there are situations and circumstances that have a way of dismissing any comfortable understanding of God. "My God, My God, why have You forsaken Me?"

In a painful place Jesus does something for us that never comes easy. He helps us by providing redemptive language that can be used by all who have to spend time in a painful place. The big issue has to do with what to say when darkness covers your life, family drops you, friends desert you, people falsely accuse you, the system lynches you, bad people taunt you, and God seems to have forsaken you.

Years ago, while serving in Nashville, I was privileged to listen to Dr. Gardner C. Taylor preach for a whole week. I was in awe at how Dr.

"ONE OF THE MOST DAMAGING ACTS TO OUR HUMANITY IS TO DENY HOW WE FEEL."

Taylor brought such piercing insight to the biblical text. I shall never forget one statement he uttered during that marvelous week of homiletical genius. Dr. Taylor said, "We, humans, can deal with just about anything but the absence of God." What do we do when life has been so painfully disrupted where the presence of God is impossible to detect? "My God, My God, why have you forsaken Me?"

In giving promising speech to a painful place, Jesus helps us by pointing out the significance of expressing how we feel. Knowing how we feel has to do with claiming our condition. I know that much is said that negates human feelings, but being real and claiming our true feelings is the only way to our true humanity. To live with distorted feelings about ourselves is to literally distort ourselves. Within the apocryphal writings of the Gospel of Thomas, Jesus said these words: "If you bring forth what is within you, what you bring forth will save you. If you do not bring forth what is within you, what you do not bring forth will destroy you." Jesus brought forth what was within Him. The combination of being dropped by family, deserted by friends, falsely accused, ganged upon by an unjust system, nailed on The Cross, all for just trying to be true to his God, made Him feel forsaken. How else could He have felt when where He was came as a result of where He believed God was? He was a victim of hate because of a belief in a God of love. Jesus felt forsaken!

One of the most damaging acts to our humanity is to deny how we feel. Black people have made an art of denying how we feel. You ask ten black people how they feel, and at least nine of the ten will tell you, "I'm fine." With all the hell that I know black people catch just for being black, how can all of us be doing so fine? We have packaged our denial of feelings into a commodity called being cool. Being "cool" is a slick way of denying how we really feel. Black men who have never been given the okay to feel anything have become cool to anesthetize deep pain. In the process of being cool, we lose the capacity to express anything other than anger in a dishonest way of disguising our pain.

Jesus identified His pain and gave voice to it. "I'm feeling forsaken. I'm feeling left alone. My pain is that of alienation, humiliation, isolation, and desolation. My pain has to do with what I believed most about God, goodness, and the way life ought to be. "Why God, have you forsaken Me?" Some of us here could set in motion the power of God's resurrection by just being honest about our feelings. We could begin the process of our own healing by just giving expression to our pain, our losses, our grief, and our despair. What is it we can say that God would not understand? (I even believe God understands "cussing.") Jesus helps us because He has identified with our pain. "He was wounded for our transgressions, he was bruised for our iniquities, the chastisement of our peace was upon him, and by his stripes are we healed."[14]

In giving promising speech in a painful place, Jesus still claimed a relationship. The very first words of this painful utterance are words of an assumed relationship. "My God, My God." The One who once claimed that "The Father and I are one," and "when you see me you see the Father," held ever so strongly to His relationship with God. Even while smitten with the acute feeling of utter abandonment, Jesus assumed that the relationship was intact. He does not throw out the words "To Whom It May Concern." No! He addressed His words to Someone with whom He had a relationship. It was as if God may have forsaken Him, but He was not about to forsake God.

Nothing has damaged us so severely

than our inability to nurture and uphold relationships. We find it hard expressing our true feelings with anyone. Something very evil in this world has perpetuated a lie that no one really cares about how we really feel. We guard ourselves and wear masks in order to protect ourselves from one another. So many of us have dismissed the entire human race because one person did us wrong. Some of us have no one to talk to about issues that are close and personal because years ago we shared with someone and what we shared was used against us. I know some men who have given up on the entire female gender because of lingering hurts from one relationship. Many black women dog all black men because of lingering hurts from one relationship.

Jesus helps us out of this painful dilemma. Just because one person, or several people let us down, God has some more people. More importantly, when life pushes us to the place where even God seems to have left the scene, remember, "Nothing (not even Crosses) can ever separate us from the love of God." Oh, I know life has many painful places. Loved ones die. People can come after us for no reason whatsoever. Those who we have depended upon can let us down. Just being who we are can get us crucified, and all of what we believe about the goodness of God becomes suspect.

Let us claim a relationship that was

established in the beginning, before our
troubles ever began, before we ever arrived
in this painful place. "My God, My God! You
have always been with me, through thick and
thin, good times and bad times. It may feel like
you have left me, but I cannot put my feelings
above You. You are greater than my feelings,
and You are My God. You are mine, because I
belong to You."

I know how hard it is for us to dismiss some
of the things we learned about God as children.
One of the things that we learned about God,
which I suspect was taught to us by oppressive
white folks to uphold unjust structures, was
to never question God. In the impressionable
years of our youth we were taught to never
question God. Whoever began that unhealthy
approach to relating with God never paused
at The Cross. At The Cross, we hear Jesus
questioning God. In a painful place Jesus asked,
"My God, My God, why have You forsaken
Me?"

I don't care how you look at "why," it is
an adverb used to interrogate. Jesus asked
God, "Why? Here I am in this painful place.
My family has dropped me. My friends have
deserted me. Enemies have conspired against
me. I have been falsely accused, ridiculed
and scorned. I have been victimized by unjust
structures and lynched by discriminating
systems. I am now being crucified on a cross, a

symbol of shame. God, I don't mean any harm, but I need to know why. It doesn't make sense to me, but if it makes any to you, please tell me why."

Brothers and sisters, I don't know how you feel about it, but I believe that Jesus asked the question because God had an answer. We may not be able to answer why we have to cry sometimes, but God has an answer. We may not know why we have to hurt sometimes, but God has an answer. We may not know why trouble is in our lives, but God has an answer. We may not understand the meaning behind a painful place, but God has an answer. It may not make any sense to us, but somewhere behind the scene, God is working on something. We may not see our way out of some dark and painful place, but God has an answer. God may not answer when I want Him to, but that's all right. I know that any question I have, God has an answer. He might not answer on a dark Friday. He may not answer on a lifeless Saturday. He may not answer during the night, but early some Resurrection morning, God will give His answer. His answer will be in spite of your painful place, all power in heaven and earth is in His hand. Hallelujah! Praise His name!

5

THE FIFTH WORD:

The Challenge of the Thirsty Stranger

"After this, Jesus, knowing that all things were now accomplished, that the Scripture might be fulfilled, said 'I thirst!' Now a vessel full of sour wine was sitting there; and they filled a sponge with sour wine, put it on hysop, and put it to His mouth."(John 19:28-29)

There is packed within the lofty Christology of the book of Hebrews an often quoted, but lightly regarded admonition. It says, "Be not forgetful to entertain strangers: for thereby some have entertained angels unaware."[15] We are prompted to consider how messengers from God can enter into our lives as total strangers, and if we are not careful we will mistreat God's messengers. This is not new. It happens all the time. Preachers are often treated as strangers, even after long pastoral tenure. People can come in our midst with a hot word from heaven but be dismissed as insignificant strangers.

If mere message bearers can be so tritely dismissed and categorized as strangers, listed as aliens or foreigners, surely the Messiah of God risks being perceived as a stranger. The messenger merely brings the message, whereas the Messiah is the message. Whatever else this ugly scene at The Cross reveals, it shows the mistreatment of One whom they really did not know.

A moving song out of our experience, now rarely sung during Christmas, says, "Sweet little Jesus boy, we really did not know who you were." No one, not even Jesus' closest acquaintances, knew who Jesus really was. The Johanine testimony begins with the assertion, "He came to His own, and those who were His own knew Him not."[16] Certainly, those who crucified Him really did not know who He was. The Sanhedrin council, watchdogs of religious order, did not know who he was. The Pharisees, with all

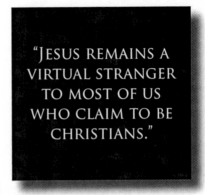

"JESUS REMAINS A VIRTUAL STRANGER TO MOST OF US WHO CLAIM TO BE CHRISTIANS."

of their fervor for Jewish nationalism, did not know who He was. The Sadducees, strapped in Jewish conservatism, not even they knew who He was. And surely we do not see it possible for Pilate, a pawn of the Roman government, to know who Jesus was.

Moreover, when we capture the spirit of our ancient song, "we really don't know who You were." I hasten to say that in 1999 [even 2004], in most communities with Christian intentions, Jesus is a stranger. In Brooklyn, a borough of Christian churches, Jesus remains a virtual stranger. If the Lord would come in our midst, I am afraid we really wouldn't know Him. If He stopped by some of our steepled castles and tarried among the comforts of our anemic expressions of faith, we wouldn't know Him. If perchance He looked in upon us and saw us with our boom-box-sized Bibles, holy robes, and ecclesial airs, we wouldn't know Him. And dare He look in upon us on any given Easter

Sunday and gaze upon those who identify with Him by adorning petticoats and bonnets, shiny suits and pointed shoes, Easter baskets and Easter eggs, we would not only not know Him, He wouldn't know us. Jesus remains a virtual stranger to most of us who claim to be Christians.

There is no way we can claim to know Him with our rampant lack of love, haughty dispositions, non-spiritual demeanors, selfish inclinations, and petty postures. We really don't know Who He is.

Jesus' words, "I thirst," draws us into what we most seek to avoid about Jesus. "I thirst" anchors upon the incarnational fact of Jesus' humanity. "I thirst" pulls us to the pulse of what it means to be a human being. "I thirst" lifts up before us the radical intention of the incarnation. "I thirst" focuses us upon the divine ideal of humanity being real. "I thirst" are the words of One who challenges us to experience the gospel in a way that liberates us to be human. "I thirst" taps into a transforming divinity that makes possible a redeemed and redemptive humanity.

Centuries ago a heresy spread throughout the Christian community that sought to deny the humanity of Jesus. Arianism promoted the notion of Jesus not being fully human. A large contingency of the church bought into the idea of a Christ who was something other than human. The pain of this word from The Cross grows out of the church's insistence to make Jesus something other than like us. The church's perversion of Christ promotes the perversions of our humanity. Even now, traces of the stench of Arianism can be detected within the Christian community.

We have a difficult time accepting Jesus' humanity. We can't deal with a Jesus who is just like us, even when our Bible tells us, "*the Word became flesh and dwelt among us.*"[17] When Jesus is viewed as supra-human, something other than human, we in turn promote our own inhumanity. The ugliest expressions of sin in our world have historically come from those who lift up Jesus to be something other than human. The institution of slavery was perpetuated by Christians who lifted up an inhuman Christ. As a result, the slaveholders viewed themselves as being more than human while they relegated slaves to being less than human.

Do you not know that at one point in our nation's history the leaders of our country pondered ways to solve the "problem of the Negro," by exterminating all blacks on American soil? Christian senators and congressman brought to the table of legislation a plan to kill every black American. Point out an expression of our humanity, and we will find either human beings trying to be more than human or people being less than human. Racism and sexism are the twins of a church that has birthed an inhuman Christ. Our young people, who now violently destroy communities, give further signals of our inability to flesh out our humanity.

The impotence of our Christian witness is the result of our placing Jesus outside of the realms of our humanity. With Jesus being outside the realm of humanity, we find religious reason to not engage in the redemption of our own humanity. Since Jesus is not like me, I don't have to involve myself in a movement to bring people into a liberating relationship with God. Since Jesus is so unlike me, I can excuse myself from the battlefields of injustice. Since Jesus is not like me, I need not concern myself with all of the problems in the black community. On the other hand, since Jesus is so unlike me, I can so easily find myself trying to be more than I actually am. Much of the arrogance of our Christian witness is the result of a warped and perverted Christology.

A recent movie entitled, "Malice," dramatized the perverted notion of a doctor who had a "god-complex." The doctor viewed himself as something other than human, someone who was equal to God. As I looked at the movie, I thought of how the Christian community has been so traumatized by what Professor Anthony Campolo calls the "Messiah complex." Unfortunately a lot of preachers view themselves as saviors. We believe we can correct all wrong, fix all that's broken, cure all who are sick, and do all that needs to be done. One of our

"ON THE CROSS HANGS ONE WHO SOBERS ALL DEVIATIONS FROM OUR HUMANITY."

conventions now has several men who all claim God has called them to be president. It is a denominational ploy to make God look confused. I sometimes suspect God may have long written off conventions as a viable vehicle for redemption.

However, nonetheless, but, notwithstanding, nevertheless, on The Cross hangs One who sobers all deviations from our humanity. He challenges us with a word fixed in the human situation. "I thirst." He did not say, "I am hungry." Nor did He say, "I'm hurting." Of all the things He could have drawn attention to, He cut through to what is essential. He centered upon the most basic of human experiences: "I thirst." He ushers our attention to the most fundamental of human needs: "I thirst."

I spent a part of my life in the South. My parents are both Southerners. I have noted a common expression of Southern hospitality is to offer visitors something to drink. If Southern folk don't have any food nor even a beverage, a cool drink of water is offered. Southerners understand that whatever else the human body may need, it will need something to drink.

"I thirst." It appears, according to the great Southern preacher, Carlyle Marney, that Jesus had an obsession with thirst. In another writer's testimony, Jesus said, "Blessed are they which do hunger and thirst after righteousness; for they shall be filled."[18] In this very gospel, the gospel of John, His first miracle had to do with creating good wine for a thirsty crowd.[19] Later on in John, we hear Him saying, "Whosoever drinks of the water that I shall give shall never thirst; but the water that I shall give shall be in you a well of water springing up into everlasting life."[20] "He that believes on me shall never thirst." He said, "If any man thirst, let him come unto me, and drink." He began His outreach ministry in a strange place, saying to a Samaritan woman, "Give me a drink."[21] He ended His ministry on a cross, as a stranger, crying out to an estranged world, "I thirst."

What then might the challenges of this thirsty stranger be for us? The first challenge of the thirsty stranger is for us to understand that in the midst of our own suffering, we can live hopeful lives. The text suggests that a sense of redemptive accomplishment came over Jesus. "Jesus knowing that all things had already been achieved, in order that the Scripture might be fulfilled, said, "I thirst." Jesus's pain and suffering did not numb Him with despair. He sensed that His suffering had to do with the hopeful longings of His people. His thirst was a continuation, in fact the summation of Psalm 69, where Israel's suffering dimmed not their hope.

Marney further noted that a lot of crosses have been erected in history. The Roman practice of execution littered the roads with crosses. In fact, mention is made of two thieves being crucified alongside Jesus. The difference in Jesus's cross and all other crosses was that Jesus's cross did not negate His future. In spite of the nails, the crown of thorns, the spear pierced in His side, the forsaken experience, Jesus still had a future.

Some of us are suffering right now. We, too, feel the pain of living in a society that doesn't seem to know us. We still feel the loneliness of that song: "Sometimes I feel like a motherless child, a long way from home." We experience the nails of a culture that seeks to confine and oppress. We even suffer personal pains and family hurts. Yet, in spite of our suffering, we can live hopeful lives.

Crosses don't kill our thirst for hope. Suffering does not need to cancel out our longing for a better day. Our pains and difficulties need not deny us of our longings for a fair and just world. Yes, we can suffer now, but we hold to a faith that says, "Blessed are those who hunger and thirst for righteousness: for they shall be filled."[22] I thirst. Do you thirst? Do you hold to the hope that we shall overcome someday?

Second, the challenge of the thirsty stranger is to understand that hopeful living begins when we address the most basic human needs. "I thirst" is an appeal to satisfy a basic human need. Even on The Cross, Jesus sought to impact upon us that good religion is simple – deal with basic human needs! How complex we have made the faith with all of our big ideas. We have bigger ideas than we have resources to achieve them. Yet, big ideas and meager resources often lead us to great despair. However, Jesus calls us to hopeful living in the addressing of basic human needs.

I love to wrestle with ideas. I often spend a lot of time and energy wrestling with lofty sermon ideas. Yet, my most hopeful moments have been when I sensed that I was helpful in getting in touch with a basic human need. I have been more hopefully lifted when someone thanks me, not for what I said, but for listening to what they had to say. I have felt more in touch with ministry, not when I did anything, but when I was just present and really seemed to care.

Brothers and sisters, the world will not be

saved by our big notions and bigger buildings. The world will be saved when we can instill hope in the lives of those struggling with their basic humanity. New York, with all of its tall buildings and big-budget items, is most hurt by the hopeless stares of those struggling for basic human needs. People are not dying from big ideas. People are dying from no ideas. Our people have no idea that the hope of this world is in how we treat the least among us. Yet, this thirsty stranger said, "For I was hungry, and you gave me something to eat; I was thirsty, and you gave me drink; I was a stranger, and you invited me in; naked, and you clothed me; I was sick and you visited me; I was in prison, and you came to me."[23]

The Bible informs us that there was no water. Jesus was thirsty at a place that had no water. The testimony is that a jar of wine vinegar (cheap wine) was there, so they soaked a sponge in it, put the sponge on a stalk of hyssop, and lifted it to Jesus' lips. We have a song that hauntingly asks the question, "Were you there when they crucified my Lord?" I sense that the intention of that song is to mystically escort us to the foot of the Cross. I don't know where at The Cross you might want to be. I don't know what role you would play at the Cross of Jesus. It may be that most of us would not want to be anywhere near The Cross. We may struggle to take the words of a

Savior who was so humanely weak that He had to cry out, "I thirst."

But for me, I wish I could have been there. For if I would have been there, I would have wanted to be among those who pieced together what they had and gave Him a drink. For I hear from the words of the thirsty stranger that in the addressing of basic human needs, we are privileged to be brought before the awesome presence of God who showed up in the humanity of Jesus. He drinks when we touch someone with compassion. He drinks when we show someone we care. He drinks when we love not wanting anything in return. He drinks when we forgive one another. He drinks when we help someone along the way. In Jesus Christ, the needy One, comes the power of God – the Saving One. And when God shows up, the stranger becomes Savior.

Give Him a drink and He's no longer a stranger, but He's a friend who sticks closer than a brother.

Give Him a drink, and He's no longer a stranger. He's the Prince of Peace.

Give Him a drink, and He's no longer a stranger. He's a burden bearer and a heavy load sharer.

Give Him a drink, and He's no longer a stranger. He's a Lily of the Valley.

Give Him a drink, and He's no longer a stranger. He's Lord of Lords and King of King.

6

THE SIXTH WORD:

Celebrative Communication

"So when Jesus had received the sour wine, He said, 'It is finished!' And bowing His head, He gave up His spirit."(John 19:30)

Communication is one of the greatest blessings of being a human being. Good communication is possibly one of the greatest gifts we can give to one another. To really know that you are understood and can be understanding can be an exhilarating experience. By the size of our phone bills, many of us have placed a high premium on communication. Whether we Christians know it or not, but fundamental to the church's mission, is to communicate the love of God to a sin-sick world. In the midst of everything we do, there ought to be the distinct message that "God so loved the world that He gave His only begotten Son, and whosoever believes in Him shall not perish, but shall have everlasting life."[24] The church exists to proclaim celebrative communication to a hell-bent world, even when we are in the midst of catching hell ourselves.

What pulls us to this awful scene on Calvary is the challenge of One who proclaims celebrative communication, even while catching hell Himself. God has organized the events of our resurrection faith that we can't even get to the bright morning of Sunday without first dealing with the dark afternoon of Friday. We cannot even get to the part we shout about without first dealing with that which we shy around. The enigmatic preacher, Carlyle Marney, has accurately stated that we cannot

even receive His resurrection without first
dealing with His crucifixion. Calvary is the
place where Jesus caught the full blows of
hell. The conspiratorial forces of hell ganged
up on Jesus at Calvary, but even within the
context of hell's fury Jesus lifted up celebrative
communication.

In basic communication there are three
primary elements. There is, first of all, the
addressor, the one who communicates. Then
there is the addressee, the one who is being
communicated to. And between the addressor
and the addressee is the address, the message
that is being communicated. When I applied this
simple communication grid to the Seven Last
Words of Jesus the discovery was amazing.
I discovered that the First Word was clearly
addressed to God, "Father, forgive them for
they know not what they do." The Second
Word was addressed to a repentant criminal,
"Today you will be with Me in Paradise."
The Third Word was addressed to the ragged
remnants of the faith community, the church,
"Woman, behold your son! Son, behold your
mother!" The Fourth Word was addressed to
God again, "Father, why has thou forsaken
me?" The Fifth Word was addressed to our
basic humanity "I thirst." The Seventh Word
was again addressed to God, "Father, into
your hands I commend my spirit." The grid
reveals God being addressed at the beginning,

middle, and end. However, the Sixth Word, "It is finished!" is an announcement that Jesus seems to have addressed to Himself. Jesus was so in touch with Himself that He could speak to Himself.

Folk normally consider people who talk to themselves as crazy. The Sixth Word represents the Savior, at the point of death, affirming to Himself that His life has been fulfilled. Throughout the pericope that includes verses 28–30, one word dominates the message. "Knowing that all things were now accomplished, that the Scripture might be fulfilled." And then "It is finished!"

The word used for accomplished, fulfilled, and finish is *telos*. *Telos* is the Greek word used to denote fulfillment or purpose. When Jesus said, "It is finished," He understood that His life had a purpose, and He had fulfilled it. Anyone who can come to the end of his or her life, after squaring things away with God, enemies, family, and community, and then announce, "It is finished" engages in celebrative communication.

I hope it does not make anyone too nervous, but I have mused over what kind of communication you or I would issue forth at our dying hour. Please don't put your brain on fast-forward and begin preparing a speech. Who would you address in your dying hour? Would you be able to clear the slate and finally get to yourself and say, "It is finished"? Most of us have a hard time squaring things with others, let alone getting right with God and ourselves. All of us have some Dark Friday personalities that we must deal with before we can claim, "It is finished!"

We have some enemies we need to forgive. We have some non-deserving folks who need extensions of grace. We all have family members and church members who can only be reconciled through our mediation. And, surely we all must clear the slate with God in the beginning, middle, and at the end. "It is finished!" None of us will be able to bootleg ourselves to Easter morning without first facing up to Friday afternoon. We have to somehow proclaim celebrative communication, even while we are catching hell.

We, preachers, have done our people a disservice by using this text for religious escape. To suggest that this text is the Christian's escape from the hardships of life is not only bad exegesis or isegesis, but grossly misleading. John's portrait of Jesus is one "who must work the works of Him who sent Him."[25] Jesus' words on The Cross are the words of One who engaged life responsibly, loved people dearly, endured pain bravely, faced evil courageously, and faced death victoriously. "It is finished" are the words of one who was aware that life has purpose when knitted to the plans of God, and God can be trusted, particularly when you are catching hell.

As I travel and consult churches, it is absolutely amazing that the majority of our churches have no specific reason for existing. We all claim to be witnesses for the Lord, but we are not really clear on how God is trying to use us to do that. We lack a clear sense of why are we here on this planet at this time. The reason why our churches lack a clear sense of purpose is because we, as a people, lack one. We all want to hear the Lord say, "Well done, good and faithful servant," but we are not always clear on what we are supposed to do, nor how we have been faithful.

I recently met a brilliant young man. At age twenty-four he had graduated from Harvard Medical School and was a practicing M.D. At age thirty-five, he had hung up his medical bag and started editing books. I told the young man he was crazy. He replied that he had finally found something fulfilling in life.

How many young people are stumbling through Brooklyn, pants baggy and drooping, skirts short and tight, with no sense of purpose? How many adults have reduced their lives to "paying the rent"? How many Christians are just going through the motions of liturgy and litany and religious formalities? There is no sense of "*telos*" gripping us as a people.

I had a hard time preparing this sermon because I did not want to engage in some preaching contest, nor did I want to discount what Jesus was really saying. I

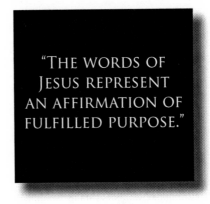

"THE WORDS OF JESUS REPRESENT AN AFFIRMATION OF FULFILLED PURPOSE."

wanted God to put us in touch with the struggle of Jesus, so that we might get in touch with our own struggles. If we are to be faithful followers of Jesus Christ, we need to tap into His words so that we, too, can issue forth celebrative communication.

If, in fact, the words of Jesus represent an affirmation of fulfilled purpose, Jesus brings us to this point by being true to himself. "It is finished" celebrates the fact that Jesus completed the assignment by being true to Himself.

One of the reasons why Jesus was known as being without sin was the fact that he never got involved in self-deceit. Reverend Mack King Carter, a Florida preacher, shared with a group of us, preachers, from the wisdom of his grandmother. Reverend Carter told us that his grandmother said, "The reason Jesus' ministry was so effective was that He didn't want to be nobody." Sin always erects fig leaves of self-deceit, pushing us to become something we are not. Jesus' victory over temptation was essentially a determination to be who God wanted Him to be.

Maybe some of you have never noticed, but Jesus never talked negative about Himself. He was so true to Himself that He always proclaimed Himself in terms of "I am." "I am the bread of life." "I am the truth and the life." "I am the way." "I am the good shepherd." "I am the true vine." "I am the bright and morning star." "I am the light of the world." "Before Abraham was I am." Jesus never said, "I ain't."

This is a good exercise for many of us to get clear on who we are, so that we might be true to ourselves. My homiletic professor, Dr. David Buttrick, once wrote that inauthenticity is the single most devastating temptation of ministry. We preachers struggle with being real. We yearn for self-justification rather than justification by grace alone. Knowing who we are will do much to assure that we fulfill the grand purposes of our lives. Knowing who we are will get us focused and galvanize our energies to greater effectiveness. God has placed us all here for some noble purpose. None of us are here just to take up space. We need to discover who we are so that we can be who God wants us to be. When we know who we are, we can face Dark Fridays, even death, and say courageously, "It is finished!"

Jesus affirmed the fulfillment of his purpose by living a life totally dependent upon God. Jesus' life from the beginning, in the middle, and even the end revealed a person totally dependent upon God. John's testimony of Jesus starts by saying, "In the beginning was the Word, and the Word was with God, and the Word was God. The same was in the beginning with God."[26] Jesus' life was so dependent on God that he became known as God in flesh. "And the Word became flesh and dwelt among us."[27]

Brothers and Sisters, a life totally dependent upon God reveals God in flesh. God can show up in you and me, be seen working in you and me, when we depend upon Him. Jesus had no earthly birthright to boast on. He was born in a manger. Jesus had no riches bequeathed to him, for he said, "the birds have nests and the foxes have holes, but the Son of Man has nowhere to lay his head."[28] Jesus had no friends he could truly depend upon, "for they all forsook Him." His family members held him in suspicion. He had no political pull, for a warrant was on Him at birth, and no one represented Him at His death. He held no favored position within the synagogues, for He was accused of keeping company with sinners and tax collectors. He depended on God.

Jesus had no artificial props to validate His life. From His own lips He said, "I must work the works of Him who sent me."[29] "My meat is to do the will of Him who sent Me."[30] "I and my Father are One."[31] "I can do nothing of myself."[32] "My Father, who has given them to Me, is greater than all, and no one is able to snatch them out of My Father's hand."[33] "Father, the hour has come. Glorify Your Son, that Your son may glorify You."[34]

The Bible further informs us that when Jesus said, "It is finished," He bowed His head and gave up His spirit." To live a fulfilled life is to recognize that all life comes from God, and the best life is one that depends on God. "It is finished" is the celebrative summation of those who anchored their lives in God. It is much easier to give God your life in death when you gave it to Him in life.

Jesus' words affirm the fact that His life's purpose had been fulfilled. His words reveal a dogged dependence on God. However, when He says, "It is finished," He suggests something else. It is suggested that what Jesus finished, started something new for you and me. Let me illustrate: I once had a suit made. I picked out the material and style, and gave the tailor my measurements. The tailor applied his trade to the materials and the pattern. He took the material and cut it into varied shapes and pieces. He then sewed the pieces together into a beautiful suit. He called me back for final alterations. He later called and said, "Your

suit is finished."
As far as his part
of the work on
my suit, it was
finished; however,
the work the tailor
finished was a new
beginning for me. I
would wear a suit
that fitted me and

"WE MAY NOT SEE
BEYOND THE HELL WE
ARE CATCHING, BUT
LET'S PLACE OURSELVES
IN THE HANDS OF
GOD."

no one else. In other words, what was finished
for him was a new beginning for me.

Brothers and sisters, on Calvary a cross
was fitted to my Jesus. He was picked apart
by abuse and scorn. His garments were
gambled apart. He was taunted with cheap
wine. He was hung high and stretched wide.
He had a crown of thorns tailored to His brow.
A soldier's sword pierced Him in the side.
When evil had done its worst, the Lord made
an announcement, "It is finished!" God's best
had endured Satan's worst. "It is finished!"
Heaven's hope had outlasted hell's despair. "It
is finished!" The dark terrors of hate had lost
to the light of love. "It is finished!"

But when He gave His spirit to God, new
beginnings became possible. We may not see
beyond the hell we are catching, but let's place
ourselves in the hands of God, and who knows
what will take place?

Your cross can turn into a crown. Your

dark afternoon can turn into a bright morning. Your tears can turn to joy. Your burden can turn into your blessing. Your suffering can turn into your celebration. Your pain can turn into your praise. Your hell can turn into a hallelujah! Your tomb may turn into your altar. "It is finished!" can also mean it's just starting. What Jesus finished, I got started and you haven't seen anything yet. Hallelujah! Praise His name!

7

THE SEVENTH WORD:

Good News for People in Pain

"And when Jesus had cried out with a loud voice, He said, 'Father, into Your hands I commend My spirit.' And having said this, He breathed His last. Now when the centurion saw what had happened, he glorified God, saying, 'Certainly this was a righteous man!' And the whole crowd who came together to that sight, seeing what had been done, beat their breasts and returned. But all His acquaintances, and the women who followed Him from Galilee, stood at a distance, watching these things." (Luke 23:46-49)

"THE GOODNESS OF GOD MEETS US IN THE MOST UNLIKELY PLACES."

In order for me to be faithful to what God has revealed to me concerning the preaching ministry, I must help people to see that the goodness of God meets us in the most unlikely places. The fact that God's goodness is at work in ways in which we don't deserve must include those experiences in life that are most difficult. One most unlikely place to experience God's grace is at the Cross of Jesus. David Buttrick, the homiletic professor at Vanderbilt Divinity School, has aptly stated that the account of Christ's death has such awesome power that it should leave would-be preachers speechless.

As I pondered over the awesomeness of preaching from this text a song rose up in my spirit:

> *On a hill far away, stood an ol' rugged cross,*
> *An emblem of suffering and shame.*

As I further mused and pondered a word from the prophet Isaiah also rose up in my spirit. The prophet said, "Surely He has borne our grief and carried our sorrows;

yet we esteemed Him stricken smitten by God, and afflicted. But He was wounded for our transgressions. He was bruised for our iniquities; the chastisement for our peace was upon Him, and by His stripes we are healed."[35] Both song and scripture lift up the fact that whatever else needs to be said about The Cross, don't neglect reminding the people that it was a place of great pain. A crucified Christ was a Christ in pain.

The painful results of betrayal were highlighted at The Cross. Jesus experienced the pain of being forsaken, of being left alone to deal with who He believed to be the common foe of his comrades and people. He experienced the pain of being misunderstood, unjustly condemned, rudely mocked by insensitive crowds, and dehumanized by nameless soldiers and strangers. The Cross was preceded by the painful dispatching of thirty-nine lashes of a metal-spiked leather strap upon the naked flesh of Jesus' back. Because of the peculiar nature of Christ's person, He was further inflicted with a crown of thorns painfully forced upon His brow.

Spitting and jeering crowds heaped insult upon insult. The very people He came to save inflicted Him with the rhythmic chant, "Crucify him, crucify him!" While on the Cross, a heartless soldier, trained in the tactics of some Gulianified law enforcement, saw the need to pierce His vulnerable side with a warrior's sword, and another added insult to injury by lifting up sour wine to His mouth to quench His thirst. The pain was intensified by the seeming abandonment of God, and He cried, "My God, My God, why has thou forsaken me?" Let none of us be so quick that we neglect the fact that The Cross was a place of pain.

On a hill far away, stood an ol' rugged cross,
An emblem of suffering and shame.

Suffering and shame are constituents of pain. The very fact that the Cross of Jesus was a place of pain calls us to consider our own pain. If we believe that God's grace was operative during Jesus' suffering, could it also be true that God's grace is operative in our own suffering? The good news of The Cross provides for us good news for people in pain.

Not one of us can deny the power of pain. We may be in denial of our pain, but none of us can deny the power of pain. Pain is a very powerful determinative of human behavior. People act out of their pain. Most of us are the way we are because of some specific expression of pain. All of us of ebony hue and African descent are the heirs of a great legacy of pain. We can deny it all we want, but pain has powerfully determined the quality of life within the black community. We relate the way we do, not out of what we know, but out of our pain.

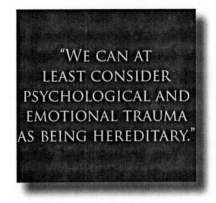

"WE CAN AT LEAST CONSIDER PSYCHOLOGICAL AND EMOTIONAL TRAUMA AS BEING HEREDITARY."

Somewhere down the road I pray God will allow me space and time to complete a manuscript entitled, Slaveshock: Discerning the Pain of the African American Family. If we accept high blood pressure and sugar diabetes as hereditary, surely we can at least consider psychological and emotional trauma as being hereditary. We have some pain that has been passed down from one generation to another. We have some inherited existential agony. We are the products of a long night of terrifying life hurts.

All of us here know at least one very intelligent person whose life has been undermined by drugs or alcohol abuse. All of us know of someone who is smart enough to know that drugs will wipe you out and too much alcohol will kill you. People don't destroy their lives on drugs because they necessarily like to be high. Drugs anesthetize people from pain. Presently, America is the most powerful country on the planet, but America has more addicted people than any other country. The only way we will ever stop the drug traffic within our communities is when we decrease the demand by being healed of our pain. The only way we can put a check on such reckless alcohol consumption is to first deal with our pain. America the beautiful is a painful place for so many people.

You, brothers and sisters, who find yourselves with one sex partner after another, you don't need that much sex! Sex addiction is just another way of anesthetizing ourselves from our pain. Huge consumption of food is a way of dealing with pain. Some of us eat everything we see as long as we see it. I saw a man who was not only several hundred pounds overweight, but he had the nerve to have a smoking habit, too. Food is primarily a source of energy, and no one needs to be walking around with an extra hundred pounds of stored-up energy.

People work all the time, workaholics, always doing something because they cannot sit down with their pain. All of this anger we spew out on people is pain-based. New York has an entire community of people who have abandoned normal living arrangements to live on the streets, on benches, or in cardboard condominiums. People don't necessarily like living outdoors, in train tunnels, or in cardboard boxes. They live as they live because pain has determined how they will live. Some of

us don't even
consider God,
consider praise
and worship, or
consider prayer
until we are
motivated by pain.
Some people don't
care anything
for a preacher

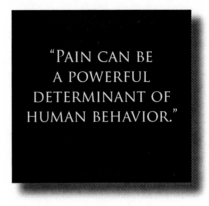

"PAIN CAN BE
A POWERFUL
DETERMINANT OF
HUMAN BEHAVIOR."

until life pushes them to have to face up to
their pain. Pain has most of the seats in our
churches filled on Sunday morning.

Some of you know what I am talking about
when I say pain can be a powerful determinant
of human behavior. "He was wounded for
our transgressions, He was bruised for our
iniquities; the chastisement of our peace
was upon Him, and by His stripes we are
healed." As Jesus died on The Cross, the Bible
even suggests that the cosmos suffered a
spasm. Nature reeled from the painful trauma
generated from The Cross. The sun was shut
down for at least three hours. The moon
hemorrhaged in blood. The holy of holies was
ruptured in two. "And when Jesus had cried out
with a loud voice, He said, 'Father, into Your
hands I commend My spirit.'

Luke noted three crowds who responded
to the pain of Jesus, yet not one of their
responses constituted good news for our pain.

One crowd saw the whole thing, and all they could do was beat their breast and return to business as usual. They sympathized with the whole painful scene, but it had no lasting impact on their lives. They went back to business as usual. A lot of people are like that. We witness pain and experience it, but it is so much easier to anesthetize ourselves with business as usual. Such actions declare, "Yes, it's sad today, but it will be okay tomorrow."

Another crowd, His own acquaintances, stood at a distance. They saw everything that happened from a distance. The very people we expect to be with us in our pain are often at a distance. Likewise, we don't like to get up close and personal to one another's pain.

Yes, the centurion glorified God. And as much as I like a good shout, the centurion does not identify with Jesus. He identified Jesus. He shouted because he came to know Jesus, but he did not feel nor did he identify with Jesus' pain. To appreciate the power of a place of pain, we need someone who identifies with the pain. What Jesus did on The Cross provided us good news for our pain.

Something needs to be said about a "cry for," a "commending to," and the "death of." The first thing Jesus did was cry out. In fact the Bible says, "He cried out with a loud voice." Of interest in Jesus' cry was that it was not a cry about, but a cry for. Again "He was wounded for. He was bruised for. The chastisement for." The Cross was not about something. The Cross was for something. A cry about something can evoke pity for others, but a cry for evokes strength from within. A cry about something may provide relief, but a cry for will pay eternal dividends.

A lot of us are into crying about something, but too few of us cry for something. It's hard accessing the power of God when all we do is cry about something, but we can get in touch with God when we cry for something. The man at the pool for thirty-eight years did a lot of crying about his pain, but he never cried for his pain.

We need to understand that God knows what is happening to us. God knows the dimensions of our pain. Our culture has discouraged crying from men, particularly from black men. As a result, men walk around with a lot of unacknowledged and unresolved pain. Perhaps what we need to do is to learn how to cry. We may need to learn how to cry for our pain rather than cry about our pain. Jesus wept about the pain of His friends in Bethany, but He cried for Jerusalem. When the crowd saw Jesus being lynched by the mob, they wept for Jesus. But Jesus said, "Don't weep for me, but weep for yourselves and for your children."[36] A cry for our pain indicates that we are in touch with it, and God dignifies those who are in touch with their pain. The grace of God can be realized when people are honest about where and why they hurt.

Earlier this year I attended a rally in support of the Diallo family.[37] I witnessed the mother of Amadou Diallo demonstrate how to cry for pain. Mrs. Diallo had just lost her son to the brutality of New York police, but she was able to put her pain in perspective. Mrs. Diallo said, "You may be wondering why I am not crying. But we are going to cry later when justice comes." She understood that a change doesn't come by just crying about pain. Redemption comes when we cry for our pain. Grace is real when we cry for our pain. "Weeping may endure for a night, but joy comes in the morning."

Something needs to be said about a commending to. The Bible says, "When Jesus had cried out with a loud voice, He said, 'Father into Your hands I commend my spirit.'" Jesus commended His spirit into the hands of God. Notice He placed His spirit into the care of His Father. He surrendered Himself into the hands of God. Lest we miss the significance of Jesus' last word, notice He says, "My spirit."

The spirit represents the true essence of a person. God is a spirit. We relate best to God, not by our bodies, but by our spirits. Did not the Lord say, "Worship God in spirit and in truth"? Did not Paul say, "We fight not against flesh and blood, but against powers and principalities, spiritual wickedness in high places"?[38] Our bodies house our spirits. Who we really are is not represented by our bodies. Who we really are is expressed in our spirits. I know some people with physical distortions who have dynamic spirits. I know some people who are not much to look at who have beautiful spirits.

The enemy took control of His body, but He maintained control of His spirit. They beat His body, but they never bruised His spirit. They tortured His body, but they never touched His spirit. They mistreated His body, but they never messed with His spirit. They brutalized His body, but they could not break His spirit. His body dripped in blood, but His spirit was draped in glory. They took His body, but He gave His spirit to God. His body was destined to a borrowed tomb, but His spirit was destined for glory.

Brothers and sisters, we are more than our pain. We are more than our trouble. We are more than our trials and tribulations. We are more than our betrayals, brokenness, and batterings. Whatever we are going through it should never control our spirit. Dr. Johnny Ray Youngblood has aptly said, "We are spiritual beings having human experiences." Human experiences can be painful, but we are more than the sum total of our pain. The late New

"WE SHOULD HAVE SOME PAIN FUNERALS."

York pastor, Harry Emerson Fosdick once said, "People may ruin your day, but never let them ruin you."

Grace says we can have earthly pain and still have heavenly protection. Yes, life often bears deep hurts! Jesus said, "Into Your hands I commend my spirit." I don't know about you, but I can vouch for God's hands. His hands are strong enough to hold back a Red Sea, but gentle enough to wipe tears from our eyes. His hands are large enough for the world, but caring enough to keep you and me. His hands are powerful enough to run the universe, but passionate enough to catch the fallen sparrow. His hands! Good news for people in pain is to place it in His hands.

The Bible says in verse 26, "And having said this, He breathed His last." Something needs to be said about the death of. Jesus died of His pains. Remember, "He was wounded for our transgressions, He was bruised for our iniquities. The chastisement of our peace was upon Him." He died of pain for our salvation.

I began by stating that pain can be a

powerful determinate of human behavior. Much
of what we do is a response to our pain. Yet,
pain need not be eternal. Some of us may not
want to bear witness, but too many of us have
wedded ourselves to our pain. We are not just
bound by our pains, but we are bound to them.
We have pain that we won't let go. We seem to
enjoy the company of our pain. Too many of us
are holding on to pain just for the sake of pain.
We have made idols of our pain. "And having
said this, he breathed His last."

Some of this pain we are nursing has
already served its purpose, and it is time to let
some pain "breathe its last." The good news
for people in pain is that there can be the death
of pain. Once we understand that in the hands
of God we are more than our pain, we should
have some pain funerals.

A couple of years ago the Devil attacked
our church. We were painfully assaulted by
the evil one. People were hurt, and I was hurt.
I sought advice from Dr. Harry S. Wright of
the Cornerstone Baptist Church. Dr. Wright
listened intently to me as I expressed my pain.
After listening he then told me a story from his
experiences at Bishop College. The late, Dr. M.
K. Curry, then president of the college called a
staff meeting. Dr. Curry saw pain in the eyes of
his staff, and he knew there was much concern
about him as a much-maligned president. Dr.
Curry candidly shared the facts of the crisis.

He told them that he had been indicted. He told them that money had been misappropriated. He then told them that some administrators had betrayed him. After he shared with them the pain of their plight, Dr. Curry said, "You all don't need to worry, because this is what I'm going to do. I am going to go home, take a shower, put on my pajamas, say my prayers, climb in my bed, and go to sleep."

With all of my legitimate pain in my eyes, Dr. Wright was suggesting to me that I go home, put on my pajamas, say my prayers, go to sleep, and let it go. What did I do? I went home that night, put on my pajamas, said my prayers, went to sleep, and let it go. In other words, once I placed my pain in the hands of God I had a funeral for it. I never lost another night's sleep because God helped me to "let it go." Again the Bible says, "And having said, this, He breathed His last." He gave it to God, and let it go.

Brothers and sisters, some of you have had some painful experiences in your life. Your childhood was painful.
Your upbringing was painful.
Your parenting was painful.
Your life has been painful.
Your relationships have been painful.
Your marriage has been painful.
Being black has been painful.
Being a woman has been painful.

Being a man has been painful.
Being in New York has been painful.
Being a Christian has been painful.
Being a preacher has been painful.
Being who you are has been painful.
Place it in God's hand and let it go!
I know it hurts, but let it go!
I know it's painful, but let it go!
I know it's been with you for a long time, but
let it go!
Let it go!
Let it go!
Let it go!

8

THE SEVENTH WORD AGAIN:

A Lesson Before Dying

"And when Jesus had cried out with a loud voice, He said, 'Father, into Your hands I commend My spirit.' And having said this, He breathed His last. Now when the centurion saw what happened he glorified God, saying, 'Certainly this was a righteous man!'" (Luke 23:46–47)

In a marvelous short novel entitled, *A Lesson Before Dying*, the late Ernest J. Gaines tells a profound story set in rural Louisiana during the late 1940s. The story centers upon a young black man named Jefferson who out of pure stupidity unwillingly witnessed the robbery and death of a white grocer. His two friends, Brother and Bear, had drunkenly drug him into a grocery store to get a bottle of wine. When the grocery store's owner refused to give them wine on credit, drunken rage and racist indignity resulted in the grocer being killed, as well as both Brother and Bear. Jefferson was the only person left alive at the scene, and he was tried and convicted of first-degree robbery and murder.

During the trial, his defense attorney argued that Jefferson was indeed innocent; however, his defense argument was based on a cruel, dehumanizing, and racist opinion held of Jefferson. Jefferson's attorney argued:

"Gentlemen of the jury, look at him – look at this. Do you see a man sitting here? Do you see a man sitting here? I ask you, I implore you, look carefully – do you see a man sitting here? Look at the shape of his skull, this face as flat as the palm of my hand – look deeply into his eyes. Do you see a modicum of intelligence? Do you see anyone here who could plan a murder, a robbery, can plan, can plan, can plan anything? A cornered animal to strike quickly

out of fear, a trait inherited from his ancestors
of the blackest Africa – yes, yes, that he can
do, but to plan? To plan, gentlemen of the jury?
No, gentlemen, this skull here holds no plans.
What you see is a thing that acts on command.
A thing to hold the handle of a plow, a thing
to load your bales of cotton, a thing to dig
ditches, to chop wood, to pull your corn. That
is what you see here, but do you see anything
capable of planning a robbery or a murder? He
does not even know the size of his clothes or
shoes. Ask him the name of the months of the
year. Ask him does Christmas come before
or after the Fourth of July. Mention Keats,
Byron, Scott, and see whether the eyes will
show one moment of recognition. Ask him to
describe a rose, to quote one passage from the
Constitution or the Bill of Rights. Gentlemen
of this jury, this man planned a robbery? Oh,
pardon me, I surely did not mean to insult your
intelligence by saying 'man.' Would you please
forgive me for committing such an error?"[39]

Jefferson's own attorney further suggested
that if the jury were to put him to death they
might as well put a hog in the electric chair.
His argument was to dehumanize Jefferson
out of being given the death sentence because
Jefferson was not a human.

Sitting in the audience was an old
woman, seventy-plus years old. She was the
godmother, known in the community as Aunt

Emma. She had been sitting, unmoving. She did not get up for water or to go to the bathroom. She did not hear all of the arguments of the prosecutor nor all of the argument of the defense. She heard one word. One word stuck in her mind. She heard them call her godson "hog." That one word that the defense used to label her godson set a fire in Aunt Emma's bosom.

Aunt Emma set in motion a process that her godson would not die a hog. She called on her dear friend to recruit her educated nephew to teach Jefferson how to be a man. She went to the white folks and begged permission for the teacher to have visits with Jefferson. She started cooking his favorite foods: gumbo, fried chicken, yams, and teacakes.

The word 'hog' had tragically seared such a deep wound in Jefferson that he couldn't eat, wouldn't talk, did not want to learn anything. He didn't want any fried chicken, gumbo, yams, or teacakes. He didn't want to talk. He didn't want to learn. He didn't even want to love. He internalized the belief that he was a hog.

After much struggle, love, sacrifice, and pain, Jefferson eventually responded. He learned how to read, write, and appreciate life. Moreover, he learned how to love himself and be a man. He was executed, yes! He was placed in the electric chair until death. But before he died he fulfilled the dream of his godmother. Aunt Emma had insisted, "I don't want them to kill no hog. I want a man to go to that chair, on his own two feet." Jefferson died, but before he died he learned how to be a man in a society that labeled him a hog.

The Seventh Word tells us that Jesus cried, "Father, into Your hands I commit my spirit." I hear in this last word a lesson before dying. It is the only word Jesus spoke for Himself. All the other words were aimed in other directions. His First Word aimed at His enemies. His Second Word aimed at one worse off than He – the thief. The Third Word aimed toward the church. His Fourth Word confessed a felt need. His Fifth Word was an acknowledgement of the pain of abandonment. His Sixth Word testified of a completed task. This last word is for Him. He died like He lived, putting others before Himself, but He did not neglect Himself. This last word speaks of a lesson before dying.

There are a whole lot of things many of us may never have in common, but the one thing we all share is death. We are all going to die. We may not die as tragically as Jefferson or as glorious as Jesus, but we are all going to die. Someone has said that we are not prepared to live unless we are prepared to die. Everything that lives must die.

I do not lift up death to create a mood of morbidity. I lift up death as an inevitable part of life. In fact, on this Good Friday afternoon

"OUR REAL IDENTITY IS IN DIVINITY."

we have been sitting here listening to a man die. We have been singing about a man dying. We have been preaching about a man dying. We have dramatized a man dying. We firmly believe that Jesus died for our sins. Yet, his death does not mean anything unless it teaches us something about death. It would be a tragedy that we can celebrate Jesus' death, but never learn anything before we die. As we consider Jesus' dying, what lessons can be learned before dying?

The one lesson we ought to learn is that our real identity is in divinity. The reason it was easy to crucify Jesus was the same reason it was easy to kill Jefferson. They mal–identified Him. I don't say misidentified. Misidentification is accidental. I use the term mal–identified. Mal–identified is intentional. It is purposeful. Misidentification can be harmless, but mal–identification is malicious. Those who persecuted him demonized Him. They characterized Him as something He was not. They called Him Belzebub. They called Him the Devil. They labeled Him a heretic.

They called Him a troublemaker. In the eyes of society they slandered His identity, therefore, reducing His humanity.

African Americans know something about that. We have been mal-identified. The mistreatment of black people by white people is made easy when black people's humanity is reduced. It is easier to shoot a "nigger" than it is to shoot a man. It is easier to kill a "coon" than it is to kill a man. In fact, we have perpetuated the mal-identification process. We mal-identify ourselves. We reduce one another's humanity. It's easier to beat a "bitch" than it is to beat a woman. It's easier to disrespect and mistreat a "dawg" than it is to disrespect and mistreat a man. Even now we have made it much too easy to reduce one another's humanity because we think it's cool to refer to one another as "dawg." Sadder yet is when we link who we are with what we have, or don't have.

In the midst of mal-identification, Jesus knew who He was. People didn't treat Him like the Son of God, but He knew who He was. People did not treat Him like the only begotten, but He knew who He was. "Father, into thy hands I commit my spirit." He had a relationship with divinity that was not erased by the insanity of His culture. Likewise my brother and sister, our real identity is in divinity. We are all created in the image and

"THE REAL 'IT' IS IN THE SPIRIT."

likeness of God. The greeting used here at Saint Paul, "Namaste,", literally affirms the divinity in each one of us. It does not matter what the world calls us, we ought to know who we are before we die. We are not hogs. We are not dogs. We are children of God. Our fore-parents were treated worse than Jefferson and they still sang, "I know I am a child a God."

A lesson before dying ought to also be that the real "it" is in the spirit. Jesus said, "Father, into Your hands I commit my spirit." The enemy took His body. They arrested His body. They whipped His body. They slapped His body. They crucified His body. They lifted His body high and stretched it wide. They pierced His body with a sword. They crowned His body with thorns. Evil inflicted its worst upon His body, but could not touch His spirit. Jesus understood that the real "it" was in His spirit.

We put a lot of emphasis in our bodies. We love our bodies, and the bodies of other people often determine how we treat people. Most of us can't even worship God until we get something special for our bodies. We may not have a prayer, a song, or a testimony, but we will have a new dress. Our closets are bursting because we believe our bodies are "it." We feed it. We oil it. We put lotion on it. We rest it. We sex it. We protect it. Some of us exercise it. We pay doctors to check it, poke it, and stroke it. We drug it. We love for someone to hug it and love it. Yet the real "it" is the spirit.

It is quite amazing that many long-time believers expect that after their bodies have been broken down with age, eaten up with disease, finalized in death, embalmed for a funeral, buried in a grave, and decomposed back to death that when Jesus comes our bodies are going to resurrect from the grave. Which body? The old one, the young one, the sick one, the embalmed one, or the decomposed one? The Bible indicates that we will have a new body, a glorious body.

Brother and sister, the real "it" is the spirit. People can kill our bodies, but never let them kill our spirit. Like Jefferson we can be executed, and like Jesus crucified. Like Amadou Diallo, we may even get shot at forty-two times. Like Abner Louima, we may be viciously sodomized in a precinct of racist perversion. We may never be able to put a name brand on our behind, but the real "it" is the spirit.

Jesus' last word is: "You can kill my body, but not my spirit. You can break my bones, but not my spirit. You can crucify my body, but not my spirit. You can put my body in a grave, but my spirit will rise again." A lesson before dying is that the real "it" is the spirit.

Jesus said, "Father, into your hands I commit my spirit." When we can learn that our true identity is in divinity, and that the real "it" is the spirit, we will land in God's hands. Why was it so important to Aunt Emma for Jefferson to die a man? Aunt Emma knew Jesus. Aunt Emma understood that if Jefferson learned to be a man, he would be what God intended for him to be. Jesus died for us that we might become what God intended for us to become. Whenever we become what God intends for us we land in His hands.

Jesus told us, "The Son of Man is being betrayed into the hands of sinners."[40] The hands of sinners arrested Him. The hands of sinners bound Him. The hands of sinners beat Him. The hands of sinners stripped Him. The hands of sinners put a crown of thorns upon His head. The hands of sinners crucified Him. But when Jesus finished what the Father wanted done, He landed in the Father's hands.

God's hands are the best hands. In His hands we find peace. In His hands we find strength. In His hands we are comforted. In His hands we find love. In His hands is understanding. In His hands we find mercy. There is deliverance in His hands. There is power in His hands. As a young child I used to sing, "He's got the whole world in His hands."

A lesson before dying is to know that when I do what God wants me to do, I will always land in His hands. I might fall, but when I fall I will always land in His hands. I might slip sometime, but when I slip I will always land in His hands. I might have some sleepless nights and long, hard days, but let me land in His hands. And when I come to the end of my journey, and I have closed up hymnbook and Bible, I want to land in His hands. When I land in His hands then I can challenge death. "O death where is your sting? O grave where is your victory?"[41] I got the victory in Jesus. Hallelujah! Praise His name!

No wonder the centurion flipped the script, changed his game, and cried, "Surely this man was the Son of God." He went from being a crucifier to being a testifier. "Surely this man was the Son of God." Hallelujah! Praise His name!

PROLOGUE

Resurrection in the Home

"Now when Jesus had crossed over again by boat to the other side, a great multitude gathered to Him; and He was by the sea. And behold, one of the rulers of the synagogue came, Jairus by name. And when he saw Him, he fell at his feet and begged Him earnestly saying, 'My little daughter lies at the point of death. Come and lay your hands on her, that she may be healed, and she will live.' So Jesus went with him, and a great multitude followed Him and thronged Him. While he was still speaking, some came from the ruler of the synagogue's house who said, 'Your daughter is dead. Why trouble the Teacher any further?' As soon as Jesus heard the word that was spoken, He said to the ruler of the synagogue, 'Do not be afraid; only believe.' And He permitted no one to follow Him except Peter, James, and John the brother of James. Then He came to the house of the ruler of the synagogue, and saw a tumult and those who wept and wailed loudly. When He came in, He said to them, 'Why make this commotion and weep? The child is not dead, but sleeping.' And they ridiculed Him. But when He had put them all outside, He took the father and the mother of the child, and those who were with Him, and entered where the child was lying. Then He took the child, by the hand, and said to her, 'Talitha cumi,' which is translated,

'Little girl, I say to you arise.' Immediately the girl arose and walked, for she was twelve years of age. And they were overcome with great amazement. But He commanded them strictly that no one should know it, and said that something should be given her to eat."(Mark 5:21-24; 35-43)

A few years ago as I walked from the Saint Paul Community Baptist Church in Brooklyn, New York, where the Reverend Dr. Johnny Ray Youngblood has served as Pastor for more than twenty-five years, a young man volunteered to walk me to my car. I had just preached one of the Seven Last Words of Jesus, and I was anxious about getting to my car and going home. My car was around the corner, and this allowed time for the brother and me to talk. I shall call the brother Leroy.

Leroy may well be a familiar sight in most urban black communities. Leroy is the neighborhood drunk who still has a way of showing up at the church. On this occasion, Leroy made an interesting statement. He said, "Reverend, they can take away Thanksgiving and Christmas, just give me Easter." Once we arrived at the car, Brother Leroy then asked me to pray for him.

"Reverend, they can take away

Thanksgiving and Christmas, just give me Easter." As you can see, Leroy's words have not left me. Although Leroy may have a lot he needs to thank God for, but what he obviously needs is a resurrection. Leroy represents the masses of brothers and sisters who need a new reality to birth within their soul and rescue them from the death-dealing madness of urban living. He needs a resurrection from the tombs of daily drunkenness. With all of my seminary education and a brain filled with Christian books, I have to agree with Leroy. Some of these Christian holidays we may be able to do without, but please give me Resurrection Day. If the truth be told, Christianity is all about resurrection. We all need God's power to constantly make a new creation out of our lives as we struggle to live a life of faith in a world bent on dying.

If we could analyze the scope of Leroy's observation, we all know that no one has suffered more from Leroy's alcoholic death than his family. Leroy is married with children. No one has been affected more by his destructive behavior than his family. The deathlike realities that prevent people from being all God intends for them to be always affects the family structure. An addiction in any home affects the whole home. A sickness in any home affects the whole home. When someone is not being fulfilled in the house, the

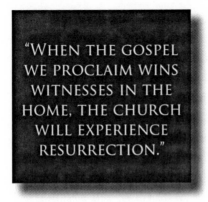

"WHEN THE GOSPEL WE PROCLAIM WINS WITNESSES IN THE HOME, THE CHURCH WILL EXPERIENCE RESURRECTION."

whole house is impoverished. Furthermore, when the Leroys of black America experience resurrection, no one will rejoice more than the family.

As the black church faces the reality that we will either live for ministry or linger in misery, I want to posit that the most crucial area for ministry is in the home. The witness of a congregation is powerfully enhanced when resurrection realities are experienced in the home. When the gospel we proclaim wins some witnesses in the home, the church will experience resurrection. Let the word get out that some of these raggedy families who emotionally maim and destroy people are experiencing resurrection, we won't have room to sit folk. Every Sunday will start looking like Easter Sunday.

The scenario that surrounds our text gives a witness to what resurrection in the home could mean. It is an incident in the life of Jesus where a man named Jairus came to see Jesus about his sick daughter. Jairus's approach is filled with the evidence of a man deeply disturbed over his daughter's condition. Jairus is noted as ruler of the synagogue. He was a leader within his religious community. Jairus represented one of Jesus' most vicious adversaries, but Jairus came to Jesus.

> "ANY CONGREGATION THAT IS NOT FACILITATING RESURRECTION WITHIN THE HOMES OF ITS MEMBERS LACKS A CREDIBLE WITNESS."

His coming to Jesus was a very unpopular thing to do. By coming to Jesus he made a statement. His coming to Jesus revealed that his religion wasn't doing anything for the condition that was troubling his family. According to his religion, he made a distasteful scene by bowing at the feet of Jesus and begging Jesus to come to his house. Jairus broke from the status quo when he went to Jesus.

Who can blame Jairus? When sickness invades one's home and the life of a loved one is hanging in the balance, it is time to do something courageous. When children's lives are at risk, it is time to take risks. When the position we hold does nothing to relieve the condition in our homes, it's time to seek a new position. We may have to change from the position of a ruler to that of a worshipper, because trouble in the home can make us do some strange things. Trouble in the home can move us from being high and lifted up to bowing down and crying out. Jairus's actions revealed that the witness of his church provided no hope of resurrection in his home. They had litany but no life, programs with no power, meetings with no mighty acts, and convention with no salvation.

Any congregation that is not facilitating resurrection realities within the homes of its members lacks a credible witness. Why should people give of their time, energy, and resources to an institution that provides nothing significant for their home? The reason people drop ten to twenty dollars on the lottery while dropping a dollar in the offering tray is because they believe the lottery will do more for their home. If the church does not demonstrate a witness where new life can be experienced, people will try something else. People read cards because of family concerns. Palms are being read because of family concerns. Cults are being created by people who are seeking answers for family crises. People are gazing at stars and interpreting astrology because of concerns for family issues. Most of the madness we witness on television is the sordid drama of family matters.

I once left the church for an extended time. In retrospect, I was not just being influenced by the sixties where all traditional authorities were being questioned. I now know that the reason I rejected the church was because it wasn't doing anything for my family. My mother and father were rushing toward an inevitable divorce. My oldest sister had been incarcerated in the juvenile system. My oldest brother was running away from home. I was skipping school and was terribly confused. The church wasn't doing a thing to resurrect new life into the home of its pastor.

Since the church wasn't helping, I did some new things. I tried some different ways. Some of the things I did were stupid, wrong, and downright ridiculous! But, people will do some stupid, wrong-headed, ridiculous things when the institution that is supposed to provide new life gives nothing but more death. When the church can do nothing but provide a soap opera atmosphere where families are destroyed by cheating, lying, backbiting, adultery, and whoremongering, people will try something else. I don't blame you, try something else!

The church is more than a gathering of well-dressed, polite-sounding, perpetrating do-gooders. The church of Jesus Christ is composed of people who have experienced resurrection. We are here because we need this resurrection faith to produce resurrection miracles in our homes.

I did a little research on Jairus. The thing that most stands out about Jairus is his name.

Jairus's name literally means "he will awaken." His name implies the resurrection. Whatever else the resurrection means, it means that "he will awaken." We are a part of a faith community that lives and breathes on the reality that death does not have the last word, but "he or she will awaken."

Notice what happens when resurrection takes place in the home. In between Jairus's request Jesus was delayed because a woman who happened to have been sick as long as the little girl was in the world touched the hem of his garment. When Jesus completed ministering to the woman, so that she might assume her family life, word came to Jairus that his daughter had died. Someone had left the context of Jairus's troubles and brought bad news and even suggested that Jairus cease from troubling Jesus.

We ought to all be rallied by Jesus' response. Jesus did not pay any attention to the bearer of bad news. The text suggests that Jesus completely discounted what the bearer of bad news reported. Jesus said, 'Do not be afraid; only believe.' The bearer of bad news tried to convince Jairus to leave Jesus. Jesus ignored his suggestion and said, 'Do not be afraid; only believe.'

First point: For resurrection to take place in the home, the church cannot listen to bad reports. The church does what is necessary

to keep Jesus' presence in the life of the
believers. Think about it! What should have
power over our members' lives, bad news
or the presence of Jesus? The resurrection
is God's way of ignoring bad news and
announcing: "He lives!" Jesus' presence in the
life of believers has a way of discounting the
power of otherwise fearful circumstances.

What the man had said may have been true,
but that is not the time to separate from Jesus.
From his perspective, she may have been
dead, but that is not the time to get away from
Jesus. All of the news coming from census
reports and government studies, which bode of
ill tidings for the black family may be true, but
this is not the time to separate from Jesus. The
budget-cutting, program-slicing agenda of the
Republicans that will certainly hurt poor people
is true, but this is not the time to be separating
from Jesus. Divorce rates are climbing at
alarming rates, particularly among Christians
and clergy. The violence and rage within our
communities, which visits every home may be
true, but this is not the time to separate from
Jesus. The terrors of addictions may be true,
but this is not the time to separate from Jesus.
The trauma of mis-education and the drama of
poor education devastate our community. All of
this may be true, but this is no time to sell out
Jesus.

As long as our homes are in the presence

of Jesus, resurrection can take place. Just as Jairus represented his home, you may have to be the lone representative of your home. Ideally the whole family needs to know the Lord, but usually one member bears the burden of keeping the family before His presence. Someone in every home needs to do all that is necessary to keep the presence of Jesus alive in the home. For when Jesus is present, fearful circumstances lose their power. When Jesus is present, trouble is put in perspective. When Jesus is present, struggles won't strain you, crosses won't break you, and graves won't bury you.

All of us know of some person who carried the faith burden of an entire family. Some faithful grandparent, mother or father just kept on living for Jesus. The whole family seemed to have been spiraling to hell, something wrong with everybody, but some faithful sister or brother just kept on walking for Jesus. Through hard trials and tribulation, suffering and sickness, pain and poverty, disappointments and disasters, they just kept on singing:

> *This little light of mine,*
> *I'm going to let it shine.*
> *All in my home,*
> *I'm going to let it shine.*

I have had experiences where I had to

funeralize faithful Christians who for the
most part kept Jesus alive in the home. Jesus
had been such a presence in their lives that
at death some family member finally got the
message, and came running, saying, 'What must
I do to be saved?'

Old man Jairus kept walking with Jesus.
When he finally arrived home there was a large
gathering of people who "wept and wailed
loudly." Jesus entered into the midst of all this
bereavement and made a disturbing comment.
Jesus said, "Why make this commotion and
weep? The child is not dead, but sleeping."
Interestingly the crowd that was so filled
with tears immediately began to laugh. They
laughed at Jesus and called him crazy.

Here is a troubling scene, for it reveals
the emotional shallowness of some people.
People can be filled with tears one minute,
but be filled with laughter the next. Such
emotional schizophrenia usually is displayed
when one challenges the validity of expressed
emotions. People can be so insincere about
the most serious matters. Jesus' response is
the only adequate one for having resurrection
experiences in the home. Jesus puts them out!

Second point: For resurrection to take place
in the home, the church should never allow
people who are playing to dominate the scene.
The church can never engage in ministry
with folk who are playing doing most of the

"WITHOUT SERIOUS DISCIPLESHIP WE ENGAGE IN CHURCH MISCHIEF."

talking, most of the voting, occupying most of the leadership positions, taking up most of the space, and deciding how the resources will be expended. God can never do a great work among fickle, wishy-washy, sometimey, off-and-on, playing-with-Jesus church folk.

Jesus put them out. He did not allow them to dominate the scene. We have to believe that some of these folk were family members. And how often do family members diminish the witness of the church? The church has been guilty of tolerating the worst kind of foolishness because so-and-so was a member of a certain family. Jesus put them all out. He took only the most concerned family members and His most serious disciples and proceeded to raise the little girl from the dead.

Brothers and sisters, serious ministry is the result of serious discipleship. Without serious discipleship we engage in church mischief. Where a church is not praying, people are playing, and the sanctuary becomes a sanctified playground. Discipleship will always eliminate mischief. And wherever there is serious discipleship, resurrection takes place. Resurrection in the home takes place when the church does not allow people who are playing to dominate the scene.

Jesus took the serious and the discipled into the room where the child was lying. The Bible says, "He took the child by the hand, and said to her, 'Little girl, I say to you arise.' My constant prayer is for the church to get serious about ministry. I pray, not for the sake of the church, but that young people in our communities can have an experience with Jesus. So many of our young girls and boys have been classified as dead. The dominant culture has written off most of our children. The so-called keepers of our society claim to have the names and addresses of the next generation of convicts. They are already saying our children are dead.

I believe that if Jesus could ever get to them, He would touch them and say, "Arise!" A major reason for me tolerating some of the foolishness of pastoring Black people is because I believe in a Jesus who says, "Arise!" In fact, the only reason I keep preaching the gospel is because I believe in a God who says, "Arise!" To every child labeled as dead, Jesus says, "Arise!" To every home shattered by a soon-to-be-dead son, or an on-your-way-to-the grave daughter, Jesus says, "Arise!"

As I hurry to the "shout," allow me to point

out one more important point. After the child
arose and began to walk, Jesus commanded
that the child be given something to eat.
He told them to give the child that which is
necessary to maintain life. It is not enough
to have our children alive and walking, we
must give our children all that is necessary
to maintain life. What that means is that
when resurrection takes place in the home,
the church should focus its resources on the
children.

If the black church is to have a glorious
future, I contend that we need to start acting
like the children need the church more than the
adults. All of what we do in the church needs
to have the children in mind. Every ministry
in the church needs to have the children in
mind. I can't speak for you, but I can speak for
myself. I know Jesus for myself. I know Jesus
raised me from the dead. I was dead in sin. I
was entombed in destruction. Jesus came into
my life and said, "Arise!" Jesus lifted me up
and turned me around. I know that I'm going to
follow Jesus for the rest of my life. I know I'm
a disciple. I know Heaven is my home.

But I have a greater concern. I need to do
all I can to make Jesus real for the children. So
I have made up my mind to use my all for the
sake of the children. I want to give what I have
so that the children will know God's Word,
experience God's love, believe in God's way,

feel God's goodness, trust God's directions,
live in God's light, and know that God cares. No
wonder the songwriter sang:

> *Jesus loves the little children,*
> *All the children of the world.*
> *Red, yellow, black, and white,*
> *They are perfect in his sight.*
> *Jesus loves the little children of the world.*

APPENDIX

A brief history of the
Saint Paul Community Baptist Church
and highlights of the ministry of
Dr. Johnny Ray Youngblood

The Saint Paul Community Baptist Church was established in 1927, when 15 worshippers formed a fellowship at 265 Thatford Avenue, in the Brownsville section of Brooklyn, New York. The Reverend S. V. Reeves was elected pastor of what was then a small storefront. Twice within the next year, the increase of worshippers made the move to larger quarters necessary. The expansion also required that the Mission receive official recognition from an independent Baptist Church. Thus, on April 1, 1929, the late Reverend Benjamin Lowry of the Zion Baptist Church of Brooklyn, New York, gave letters to 12 members of the small gathering giving consent to officially organize the St. Paul community Mission. One of the 12 members of that congregation was Edward Leonard Haywood, who assumed the role of the Mission's leader. He would eventually be installed as the pastor and served in that capacity for two years.

Due to the rapid growth of the Fellowship,

three more pastors would be called to serve St. Paul over the next 43 years. They included Reverend Elbert H. Hamblin, the Reverend Adolphus Smith and Reverend Johnny Walker. Of these, the Reverend Adolphus Smith was the most notable, having served for a period of 27 years. During his tenure, the church prospered and grew rapidly. A worship site was built from the ground up, but was later given up to accommodate urban renewal. The congregation then purchased a former athletic/social club at 1926 Prospect Place and converted it into a House of Worship. Reverend Johnny Walker succeeded the Reverend Smith following his retirement in 1965 and served the congregation for seven years.

In 1974, the congregation called to its pastorate, a young preacher, twenty-six years old at the time, in the person of Reverend Johnny Ray Youngblood. Of an approximate 250 active members, only 84 met to extend the call to the pastor. At that time, the annual operating budget was less than $18,000.

In 27 years of service to St. Paul Community, Dr. Johnny Ray Youngblood has grown the congregation from 84 members to more than 7,000 members and the annual budget has exceeded 3.5 million dollars. The church hosts three Sunday Worship experiences, 6 a.m., 8 a.m., and 11 a.m. The Midweek services, both noon and evening usually have capacity crowds and there are 25-30 weekly classes include bible study, men, women, and youth issues, a twelve-step substance abuse counseling program, alternative healing disciplines, martial arts, dance, drama, deaf ministries and many more. Pastor Youngblood currently oversees a staff of more than 60 full-time employees and a substantial group of part-timers and volunteers.

Dr. Youngblood has provided tremendous leadership in affecting positive change in the East New York area. As the leader of the East Brooklyn Congregation (EBC), an affiliate of the Industrial Areas Foundations, he has led in the construction of nearly 3,000 owner-occupied single-family homes in three of the most devastated communities in Brooklyn. The Saint Paul Community Baptist Church owns nearly all of the property in its block, including the businesses. The establishment of the Saint Paul Community Baptist Academy provides an educational alternative to a faltering public school system.

In September of 1995, Dr. Youngblood launched what has become one of the premier projects of the church's annual calendar, now known as the Commemoration of the Maafa. Dr. Youngblood is spearheading a national effort to promote the Maafa as a spiritual movement toward the healing of the nation.

The Commemoration of the Maafa pays tribute to the millions of African men, women, and children lost in the horror of the TransAtlantic Slave Trade.

In 2001, Dr. Youngblood assumed the additional task of being the pastor of the Mount Pisgah Baptist Church, Brooklyn. Mount Pisgah Baptist Church is located in Bedford Stuyvesant, the largest concentration of people of African descent in any urban setting in the world. His presence has already sparked a renewal in the church life of the community, and has been the catalyst of a miracle-reformation at Mount Pisgah. He provides sterling leadership to both Saint Paul Community and Mount Pisgah, as well as provides a model of effective leadership for urban churches. His work within the Black church has had him featured as one of the "ten most influential" New Yorkers. He has also been featured in Mirabella, Details, Emerge, and Essence Magazine. He has been featured in news journal programs on ABC's 20/20, FOX 5's McCreary Report and the Charlie Rose Show. Dr. Youngblood has courageously provided ministry in a disaster zone.

ENDNOTES

[1] Freedman, Samuel G., Upon This Rock: The Miracles of A Black Church, (Harper Collins Publishers, New York, New York, 1993) pp. 49-50.

[2] Abner Louima and Amadou Diallo were victims of race-motivated acts of police brutality. Louima was beaten and sodomized with a toilet plunger within a police precinct in Brooklyn, New York. Diallo was shot at forty-two times and fatally slain by police when he reached for his wallet on the stoop of his own home in the Bronx.

[3] John 14:6
[4] John 8:32
[5] Mark 5

[6] Henry J. Lyons was the president of the National Baptist Convention, USA, Inc., the largest denomination of African Americans in the nation. He was shamefully brought down through blatant misdeeds motivated by blind ambition and greed. Consequently, he suffered embarrassing public dredging that resulted in a federal prison conviction.

[7] Genesis 50:20
[8] Luke 23:39b
[9] 1 Corinthians 2:9
[10] Philippians 3:10

[11] A Cuban boat child who captured the attention of the American public when relatives (continued on next page) in Florida refused to return the child to his father in Cuba. The United States government eventually became involved and forcefully returned the child to his father. This was a political disaster for the Clinton Administration.

[12] John 19:26
[13] 1 Corinthians 15:19
[14] Isaiah 53:5

[15] Hebrews 13:2
[16] John 1:11
[17] John 1:14
[18] Matthew 5:6
[19] John 2:1-11
[20] John 4:13-14
[21] John 4:7
[22] Matthew 5:6
[23] Matthew 25:35-36
[24] John 3:16
[25] John 9:4
[26] John 1:1-2
[27] John 1:14
[28] Luke 9:58
[29] John 9:4
[30] John 4:34
[31] John 10:30
[32] John 8:28
[33] John 10:29
[34] John 17:1
[35] Isaiah 53:4-5
[36] Luke 23:28

[37] Amadou Diallo was an African immigrant who was brutally shot down by New York police. He was shot at forty-two times. Nineteen bullets pierced his body from the top of his head to the bottom of his feet. He was shot because he went to withdraw his wallet for identification purposes.

[38] Ephesians 6:12

[39] Gaines, Ernest J, A Lesson Before Dying, (Vintage Books, New York, N.Y. 1993), pp. 7-8.

[40] Matthew 26:45
[41] 1 Corinthians 15:55

CPSIA information can be obtained at www.ICGtesting.com
Printed in the USA
BVOW012111210911

271817BV00001B/1/A